HOMO SAPIENS

Vol. IV

AGGRESSION & HATE

Superstition, Faith, Religion, Politics

Collection of Essays

Shimon Garber

Newcomers Authors Publishing Group

2024

Shimon Garber
Homo Sapiens Vol. IV
Aggression & Hate
Collection of essays
Newcomers Authors Publishing Group
All rights reserved
© Shimon Garber

ISBN: 978-1-950-430-42-0 ; HS 4; Rus.
ISBN: 978-1-950-430-43-7; HS IV; Eng.
ISBN: 978-1-950-430-41-3: HS IV: Eng., ePub

Russian text editor: V. Serova
Translations: S. Garber
Interior Designer: Michael Grossman
Corrector: A. Pelan
Newcomers Authors Publishing Group

TX 8-821-907
2024

Contents

Preface 1
Israel On Fire 5
   Al Qaeda 5
Holocaust 9
Creation of The State of Israel 11
Israeli Wars 17
   "We're At War" 21
   Islam 26
Hamas 35
Palestinians 69
Faith-Religion-Ideology 77
   Beginning 77
Russia 93
   Karl Marx 97
   Vladimir Lenin 104
   Joseph Stalin 116
   From the CHEKA to the FSB 120
   Nikita Khrushchev 126
   Putin 136
Iran 145
   Iran's Nuclear Program 151
Biden's America 155
Afterword 161

Preface

The fourth volume of my collection of various essays is devoted to reflections on humanity: its history, development, and the unique emergence of Homo sapiens species. Various types of human species, originating in Africa about 300,000 years ago because of climate change, were forced to move in search of new food sources. The history of the development of our species, Homo sapiens, is one that is chiefly influenced by war, religion, and ideology.

War: Humans have always had a thirst for power and profit, leading to mass suffering and destruction. Wars have always been the main engine of historical development and, at the same time, a threat to the existence of human civilization.

Religion: the influence of religion on forming social foundations and worldviews. Contradictions between religious views, scientific understanding of evolution, and the impact of religious conflicts on world politics.

Ideologies and modern society: The transition from a society regulated by religious traditions to a secular model of social structure, the secularization of society (the process of reducing the role of religion in the life of society) is an irreversible process that has steadily led to a reduction in the scope of religion and will eventually lead to its progressive decline and, in the very long term, its disappearance. Judging by the influence of religion on the brain of modern man, common sense and the logic of the coexistence of different opinions and views are still incredibly far from ideal. Our species has moved from societies built on religious principles to monarchy, then to societies built on ideologies, and the latest achievement of modern civilization: democratic principles, with respect for individual rights and international law in the modern world. However, it is regrettable that our species is still far from creating an ideal community suitable for the coexistence of different races, ideologies, and religions on Earth.

Scientific advances and their consequences: Scientific discoveries, from writing to modern artificial intelligence, have created the potential to turn the world into a "Garden of Eden" but are used solely to spark new conflicts and intensify existing confrontations.

The challenges of the modern world, including nuclear threats, mass migration, and environmental disasters, highlight modern society's fragility and the need for international cooperation to prevent global disasters.

Despite all its achievements and progress, humanity, just as it did thousands of years ago, continues to face many problems that could lead to self-destruction. The primary solution is to preserve and improve living conditions on Earth. Humanity must strive for peace, mutual understanding, cooperation, and overcoming obstacles caused by wars, religious differences, and ideologies.

The need for collective efforts to overcome global challenges such as climate change, inequality, and the dangers of nuclear proliferation is clear. All this leads to the understanding that only through joint action can sustainable world development be achieved.

There is optimism about humanity's potential to make the Earth a place where future generations can live and prosper. But achieving this goal requires overcoming deep-seated prejudices and conflicts. Scientific and technological achievements can be used both for the benefit of humanity and for its destruction. It remains important to reflect on human nature and the possibility of changing it. Are human beings capable of overcoming their aggressiveness and desire for dominance to build a society based on cooperation, tolerance, and mutual respect? Success in this direction will prevent the self-destruction of humanity and allow it to reach new heights in the development of civilization.

Homo Sapiens Vol. IV is a continuation of a series of essays about the complex and unique history of human civilization: its past, present, and prospective future. We hope those who read this volume will think about their place in this world, where each of us is responsible for creating a better future for all of humanity.

Israel On Fire

Al Qaeda

On September 1, 2001, a new era began for the United States. Nineteen suicide bombers with ties to the Islamist organization Al Qaeda, led by wealthy Saudi Arabian Osama bin Laden, carried out an unprecedented attack on America that claimed the lives of 2,996 innocent people.

Nineteen Islamist terrorists, according to a plan developed by Osama bin Laden's team, armed with paper cutters, hijacked four passenger airliners and flew them to pre-designated targets.

At 8:46 a.m., the first airliner, traveling at several hundred kilometers per hour and carrying about 40,000 liters of jet fuel, crashed into the 110-story North Tower of the World Trade Center in Lower Manhattan.

At 9:03 a.m., the second airliner crashed into the 110-story South Tower. Fire and smoke flew upward. Steel, glass, ash, and bodies fell. The Twin Towers, which employed up to 50,000 people daily, collapsed in the span of 90 minutes.

At 9:43 a.m., a third airliner crashed into the east wall of the Pentagon.

At 10:03 a.m., the fourth airliner crashed into a field thanks to the heroic passengers who tried to take control of the plane.

In response to the terrorist attacks of September 11, 2001, the United States conducted a military operation in Afghanistan to destroy Al-Qaeda and ISIS (Islamic State of Iraq and the Levant), which was taking over the eastern countries.

According to intelligence reports, Osama bin Laden was hiding in the mountain caves of Afghanistan. The US Army had used the latest non-nuclear depth charges, penetrating rocks to considerable depths. Osama bin Laden fled to Pakistan. On May 2, 2011, Osama bin Laden was killed during a US Navy raid in Pakistan.

In 2003, the United States launched a war in Iraq, justifying the invasion with dubious information about Iraq's ability to produce an atomic bomb. The Iraqi government, led by Saddam Hussein, was overthrown. The invasion was linked to the war against the 9/11 terrorist attacks. No traces of the development of atomic weapons were found.

ISIS is a radical terrorist group that declared itself the "Islamic State" in 2006. ISIS has been conducting successful military operations in Syria and Iraq for several years, actively spreading the ideology of radical Islamism. Having formed itself into an organized military force, it controlled vast territories, the so-called "Islamic State" caliphate, from Afghanistan to Lebanon, in territories where up to eight million people lived. ISIS, by this point, had become a real threat to world security. International cooperation condemning brutality, human rights violations, and ISIS's stated intention to spread the war to other states to create a "Global Caliphate" prompted many countries to take military action against the terror group. By the end of 2017, the Islamic State had been destroyed. US Special Forces in Syria killed ISIS leader Abu Bakr Baghdadi.

Holocaust

There Would Not Be Happiness, But Unhappiness Helped

The Holocaust was a genocide in which Nazi Germany killed approximately six million Jews between 1941 and 1945. It was one of the most tragic and horrific crimes against humanity in history.

The Holocaust, also known as the Shoah, was a systematic, bureaucratically organized attempt to exterminate the entire Jewish population. The Nazis, seeking to create a "pure" Aryan race, considered the Jews their main enemy. Genocide was carried out through mass executions in the form of gas chambers in concentration camps, forced labor, starvation, and medical experimentation on prisoners.

The persecution of Jews began with Hitler's rise to power in 1933, and systematic extermination began with the attack on the Soviet Union on June 22, 1941, in a campaign known as Operation Barbarossa. That marked the beginning of an essential phase of the Holocaust, which included the creation of mobile killing squads known as Einsatzgruppen, which were embedded with German troops and shot Jews where they lived.

The end of the Holocaust came with the end of World War II in Europe on May 8, 1945. As Allied forces liberated Nazi-occupied areas, they discovered concentration camps and prisoners who had survived horrific conditions. The aftermath of the Holocaust had a profound impact on world history and politics, leading to the creation of organizations and laws aimed at preventing future genocides.

Jews all over the world dreamed of returning to the lands of their ancestors. The first large-scale global migration (Jews call the return to the land of their ancestors' aliyah [in Hebrew]) can be said to be the exodus of Jews from Russia from 1882 to 1903.

Creation of The State of Israel

Lord Arthur James Balfour played a vital role in the history of the creation of the State of Israel. His name is closely associated with the so-called Balfour Declaration, formulated in November 1917. That was a letter sent by Lord Balfour, then British foreign secretary, to the leader of the British Jewish community, Lord Rothschild.

This letter expressed support on behalf of the government for the creation of a "national home of the Jewish people" in Palestine, which was then under the control of the Ottoman Empire and subsequently came under the British Mandate. It is important to note that the declaration also emphasizes that nothing should infringe upon the civil and religious rights of existing non-Jewish communities in Palestine.

This declaration played a vital role in the further development of the Zionist movement and formed the basis of international support for the idea of the creation of Israel. Although issues related to the balance of interests between the Jewish and Arab populations of Palestine continued to be the subject of much debate and conflict, the Balfour Declaration significantly impacted the region's political landscape in the long term.

In 1917, Britain published the Balfour Declaration supporting the creation of a "national home for the Jewish people" in Palestine, then under Ottoman control. After World War I, Palestine came under the British Mandate, and there was an influx of Jewish immigrants to the region. World War II and the catastrophic Holocaust intensified the desire for a Jewish state, as millions of Jews lost their homes and needed a safe shelter. In 1947, amid the growing Arab-Jewish conflict and Britain's inability to govern Mandatory Palestine, the issue was referred to the United Nations. The UN proposed a plan to divide Palestine into two states: Jewish and Arab. On May 14, 1948, the day the British Mandate expired, David Ben-Gurion declared the independence of the State of Israel. That led to the first Arab-Israeli war, in which the newly formed state was able to maintain its position and even expand its territory. The creation of Israel marked a critical moment in Jewish history, providing refuge to many Jews from around the world, especially those who survived the Holocaust and were forced to flee anti-Semitic countries. However, it also exacerbated the long-standing Arab-Israeli conflict, the consequences of which are all too evident today.

Theodor Herzl, in 1897, at the First Zionist Congress in Basel, proclaimed the creation of the Zionist Organization (the movement's goal is the revival of the Jewish people and the return to their historical homeland—Israel).

British Foreign Secretary Balfour 1917 expressed support for creating "a Jewish national home in the territory of Palestine."

Contrary to the desire of the Arabs to create a single Arab state, the Middle East was parceled up between colonial states.

Palestine and Mesopotamia in 1922 were controlled by the British Crown under a mandate issued by the League of Nations. The decision of the League of Nations proclaimed the implementation of the Balfour Declaration and the creation of a "Jewish national home" in Palestine.

Zionism is a movement whose goal is to create a national state for Jews. The founders of Zionism believed that if the Jews created a state, they would be able to protect themselves. In 1948, with the assistance of the UN, the State of Israel was created on the territory where Jews lived before the expulsion by the Romans in 139 BC.

The creation of the Jewish state of Israel resulted from long historical processes, and there were many reasons behind its advent. Still, the critical point was the need to provide refuge for the Jewish people after the horrors of the Holocaust.

The State of Israel was proclaimed on May 14, 1948, on the territory of the former Mandatory Palestine. This area had historical significance for Jews even before the Christian era. In three millennia BC, this area was inhabited by Canaanite tribes. In the 13th century BC, warlike tribes (sea peoples) from the islands of the Mediterranean Sea tried to invade Egypt and the southern territories of the Mediterranean coast. They captured the territory that is today called Gaza.

In the 9th century BC, ancient Jewish tribes founded the kingdom of Israel in the territories of Canaan, which subsequently split into two states. The Kingdom of Israel is in the north, and the Kingdom of Judah is in the south. Between the Jews and the "peoples of the sea," whom the Jews called Plishtim, i.e., Philistines, there were wars for the possession of territories.

Assyria, the largest empire of the ancient world, conquered the Northern Kingdom of Israel in 722 BC. The population was driven into slavery and scattered among other nations. Under tradition, Assyria resettled other peoples to these places. The Babylonian king Nebuchadnezzar conquered the southern Kingdom of Judah in 586 BC. The Jerusalem temple was destroyed, and the population was taken prisoner and were relocated to Babylonia.

After the conquest of the Babylonian kingdom in 538 BC, the Persians, led by King Cyrus the Great, allowed all captive peoples to return to their territories. The kingdom of Judah was restored.

The Persian state fell after a battle in 334 BC. All of Asia Minor came under the rule of Alexander the Great.

After the commander's death, the conquered territories were divided by his heirs, commanders. The kingdom of Judah came under Seleucid rule. The Jews continually rebelled against the Seleucid kingdom (166–142 BC), ending with the independence of Judea.

A new player on the world stage at the time, Rome, invaded the Middle East. The Jews rebelled against their new enslavers. The Jewish Wars against Roman rule, so-called by Josephus, continued unabated.

The Jews were expelled from their country by the Romans in 139 after the suppression of the Bar Kokhba revolt. The land of Palestine is associated with the name of the Philistine people who once lived there. Scattered among numerous nations, the Jews laid the foundation of a "diaspora" (a religious-ethnic group living in foreign lands as a national-cultural minority) outside Judea.

* * *

Jews are one of the oldest peoples in the world, having survived to modern times. The history can be read both in the Bible and in extra-biblical sources. The second captivity of the Jewish people is associated with the Babylonian king Nebuchadnezzar (circa 587 BC). The Babylonian captivity in 539 BC ended, allowing Jews to return to their lands.

In 63 BC, Roman troops under the command of Pompey the Great arrived in Judea, where Jews had lived for many centuries. The Jews repeatedly resisted and rebelled against Roman rule. The Romans eventually destroyed Jerusalem, burned the second temple, and dispersed the Jewish inhabitants throughout the Roman Empire. The Roman Empire controlled vast territories, and Jews were scattered throughout all then-known countries.

Decades before the creation of the State of Israel, the idea of returning Jews to their historical homeland was actively discussed within the Zionist movement. Zionism as a political movement began to take shape in the late 19th century and aimed to create a nation-state for Jews in Palestine. Two millennia have passed, but the Jews have not forgotten their Homeland. During the celebration of the leading Jewish holiday, "Passover" (the exodus from Egypt and the formation of Jewish religious life), Jews said for two thousand years: "Next year—in Jerusalem."

Israeli Wars

Since its founding in 1948, Israel has been involved in several significant military conflicts. Each war and conflict had its specific causes, contexts, and consequences, which shaped the country's domestic and foreign policies. A brief overview of the central wars:

War of Independence (1948–1949) – began after the declaration of Israeli independence and the subsequent invasion of Arab armies from Egypt, Jordan, Syria, Lebanon, and Iraq. The war ended with a truce and a significant expansion of the areas controlled by Israel compared to the boundaries proposed by the UN in 1947.

Suez Crisis (1956) – Israel, allied with Britain and France, attacked Egypt following Egypt's nationalization of the Suez Canal. The war ended with UN intervention and the withdrawal of Israeli troops but ensured freedom of navigation for Israeli ships through the Straits of Tiran.

Six-Day War (1967) – As a result of tensions with neighboring Arab states, Israel launched a pre-emptive strike on Egypt, leading to a rapid military campaign against Egypt, Jordan, and Syria. Israel captured the Gaza Strip, Sinai, the West Bank, East Jerusalem, and the Golan Heights.

Yom Kippur War (1973) – Egypt and Syria launched a surprise attack on Israel during the Jewish holiday of Yom Kippur. After heavy fighting, Israel repelled the invasion, but this resulted in significant casualties and subsequent peace negotiations.

Lebanon War (1982) – began as an operation against Palestinian militants in southern Lebanon but developed into a prolonged military presence that caused numerous conflicts and clashes, including with Hezbollah.

Then, there were intifadas and subsequent conflicts with Hamas and other groups. Since the late 1980s, Israel has faced a series of Palestinian uprisings (intifadas) and armed clashes, including operations in the Gaza Strip in 2008–2009, 2012, and 2014.

Each of these conflicts left a significant mark on Israel's history and politics, as well as influenced its relations with neighboring countries and the world community.

Relations between Iran and Israel remained tense and hostile, with both countries regularly exchanging rhetoric and threats. Iran has often expressed support for anti-Israeli proxies such as Hezbollah in Lebanon and Hamas in the Gaza Strip, which have carried out military operations against Israel. Israel, in turn, accused Iran of seeking to develop nuclear weapons and stated that Iran poses a significant security threat to the global community. Israel has been credited with carrying out covert operations and attacks on Iranian nuclear facilities and scientists.

Israel has accused Iran of attempting direct attacks, such as using drones and missiles from Syria, where Iran supports President Bashar al-Assad. Israel responded with air strikes against

Iranian targets in Syria to prevent an Iranian military presence on its borders.

There was no direct military conflict between Iran and Israel, but both countries actively participated in regional confrontation, which included military actions, support for opposing sides, and mutual threats.

On the night of April 13, 2024, Iran launched a major military attack on Israel, the first direct attack of this magnitude. This operation involved approximately 170 drones, more than 30 cruise missiles, and more than 120 ballistic missiles. According to multiple sources, the attack targeted various locations throughout Israel and the Israeli-occupied Golan Heights.

Israel's response to the attack was robust, with its layered air defense systems, including Iron Dome, Arrow, and David's Sling, successfully intercepting about 99 percent of incoming threats before they could cause significant damage. These defensive efforts were supported by the United States, Britain, France, and Jordan, who helped mitigate the attack together.

Iran's actions were reportedly in response to a previous incident on April 1, when an Israeli airstrike on the Iranian consulate in Damascus killed two Iranian generals. This escalation reflected ongoing tensions between Israel and Iran, exacerbated by Israel's ongoing conflict with Hamas and other Iran-backed groups in the region.

The situation remains tense and has the potential for further escalation, as both countries have exchanged stern warnings about a future standoff. International reaction was mixed, with calls for restraint but also strong support for Israel's right to protection from various allies.

Israel and the surrounding Muslim countries have been at odds since the creation of the State of Israel in 1948. According to the UN plan, two states should be created on the territory of a British mandatory colony. One for Jews, one for Arabs. While Jews greeted the decision with delight and jubilation, their Arab neighbors rejected the very idea of a Jewish state in the Middle East. The first war began the day after the proclamation of the creation of the Jewish state. Modern Israel has experienced eight wars and many armed clashes in a historically short period of seventy-five years. Trying to secure its territories, Israel expanded its borders to the maximum safe distance.

The State of Israel today is under fire not only from various Islamist extremist groups but also from the UN. This organization has become a nest of detractors and opponents of sanity and freedom. The UN budget, which consists of contributions from member states of this body, amounts to billions of dollars. What are these fabulous free billions spent on?

The proposed budget for 2024 was $3.3 billion. Sooner or later, this little-respected organization will follow the League of Nations, founded after the First World War.

The State of Israel was proclaimed on May 14, 1948, on the territory of the former Mandatory Palestine. This area has historical significance for Jews even before the Christian era. For three thousand years, this territory was inhabited by Canaanite tribes. The Land of Israel is the homeland of the Jewish people. The Bible describes the history of the Jewish people, who lived in this territory for one thousand years BC. Rome, which captured these territories, expelled the Jews from this country in 139 for constant rebellion against Roman authority. In honor of the Sea

Peoples, the Philistines renamed the territories Palestine, which conquered Gaza in the 13th century BC.

"We're At War"

On Saturday, October 7, 2023, a new era began for Israel. The terrorist attack, for which the country was preparing and the prospect of which had been discussed in all media, turned out to be a complete surprise for the country's leadership. Prime Minister Benjamin Netanyahu fell into prostration, perhaps from surprise, and only came to his senses five hours later. What's surprising here? Comrade Joseph Stalin, having learned of the surprise German attack in 1941, needed several days to come to his senses. When his party colleagues came to him, he was ready to be arrested. But they came to him with the most humble request to return to power. Something similar happened in Israel. The party needed a leader. Benjamin Netanyahu, summoning all his courage five hours after the unexpected attack, addressed the people of Israel: "WE'RE AT WAR"!

On that day, the tragic Hamas attack continued for an excruciatingly long time. The terror perpetrated broke through the ceiling of pain. But the most terrible humiliation came with the debunking of the myth about the invincibility of the Israeli Defense Forces, the IDF, and the omnipotence of the Israeli intelligence services. Everything that the military, the media, and Israeli society had nurtured throughout the country's history collapsed that day.

Israel will win. No one has any doubts. The price of this victory will be extremely high. Israel must change. The dead can only be mourned. Those responsible for this tragedy will be named and convicted. A new era will dawn on Israel. An ancient country should not live by ancient laws.

Today, Israel must develop and adopt a national constitution. Israel, a modern state, cannot live by ancient religious laws in the modern world. The High Court of Justices (BAGATZ) should become the Supreme Court to monitor compliance with the Constitution.

On that October day, the tragedy continued for an impossibly long time. Israel has not experienced such casualties in a single day in the last fifty years. The terror perpetrated by Hamas broke through the ceiling of pain. Everything that the military, the media, and Israeli society had nurtured throughout the country's history collapsed that day.

The catastrophe of 10/07/2023 should make Israel an even more powerful and modern state: one where adults don't have to be worried about the younger generation.

What about those people the Israelis didn't even think about? Did they think "kids are fooling around"? Although everyone already knew everything. There are already many victims. Armed and trained in the camps of Iran and Russia, thirsty for blood and profit, ready to die and receive the promised reward in the one where seductive languid houris fulfill all desires, writhing in sensual dances, awaken the desire in martyrs of Islam, tired of love pleasures.

Moloch (the deity to whom human sacrifices were made) got his. The idea of invincibility, superiority, humanism, morality, transnationality, and a mighty Israel no longer exists. The curtain fell, revealing a terrible, impossible truth. The Arabs were not wearing slippers or sandals on bare feet but dressed in military uniforms, with AK assault rifles at the ready, on scooters, pickup trucks, and other various vehicles. With only a bulldozer as heavy equipment they destroyed the Israeli security fence in many places, an apparatus that billions of dollars had been invested in. These Arab militants humiliated the entire country. That was their goal. The entire Arab world saw this. Everyone saw everything and that it was possible. The world has seen that a motivated fighter, armed with the Islamic faith and military weapons, can dance on a tank worth four million. The world saw that an ultra-modern tanks, airplanes, and an aircraft carrier heading to the shores of Israel would also be defenseless. More precisely, useless. Almost two billion Muslims saw this.

Israeli society on October 7 lost faith that such attributes of a strong state as "the army will always be on top"; even despite the split in society, unfortunately, the country became disillusioned.

* * *

In creating the State of Israel, Jews were motivated and united by an idea and believed in unity, country, and the future. The idea of society was higher than that of the individual. And this coincided with the Torah (Old Testament). Today, the idea of serving God is prevalent in Israeli society. Twenty percent of the population serves their homeland in the army, acquires a profession, gains knowledge that allows them to understand the essence of objects and phenomena, and are informed enough to choose a profession and take their place in the modern world. For the religious sector, serving God has become a big business in Israel. That is how it always was. But the ultra-religious parties owe this to Prime Minister Benjamin Netanyahu in coming to power and having the opportunity to manage finances at their discretion.

Well-founded fears of criminal prosecution for his actions as prime minister in his previous term and a desire to secure his destiny prompted Netanyahu to change some laws and subjugate the Supreme Court (High Court).

Prime Minister Netanyahu signed a coalition agreement with ultra-religious and ultra-nationalist parties and gained the necessary advantage for power with a margin of four votes. Netanyahu again became prime minister, handing out ministerial posts to new friends in the hope of later outwitting everyone. Israel now has the most far-right government in its history.

The coalition parties immediately demanded the implementation of the concluded coalition agreements. Netanyahu said on July 20 that his government was working on the issue of judicial reform. The essence of this reform was that the Knesset (government) would have the right to overturn the Supreme Court (High Court) decisions regarding laws and government regulations. Thousands of people protested against judicial reform across the country. The police used water cannons to disperse protesters and other violators. Mass protests took place across the country. The Judiciary Reform Act has only fueled further protests following Parliament's approval of one of the most controversial reform bills, repealing the "reasonableness standard." Passed in July 2023, the law removes the ability of courts, including the Supreme Court, to challenge executive decisions that may be deemed "unreasonable."

Israel's enemies were watching what was happening. Benjamin Netanyahu found himself held hostage by his coalition partners. In the process of forming a coalition government, the prime minister was forced to make a deal with ultranationalists known for their homophobia and harsh attitudes toward Arabs. Israel's secular future, peace in the Middle East, and relations with the United States are at risk.

Following the coalition agreements, the heads of far-right parties received ministerial posts. The post of Minister of Finance was given to Bezalel Smotrich, leader of the Religious Zionist Party. Itamar Ben-Gvir, leader of the far-right Otzma Yehudid party, has taken over as Israel's Minister of National Security. He demanded the creation of a new security agency: the National Guard, which would consist of around two thousand recruits. His demand was satisfied by allocating a billion shekels to form and equip the new structure. Millions of shekels were allocated to far-right religious parties. These coalition parties demanded that Netanyahu approve gender segregation in public places. For example, separate classes for boys and girls were proposed in public schools and universities, dividing theater, concerts, and cinema halls into sectors. Israel's Orthodox community maintains strict gender segregation, including travel on public transport.

The rabbis called on religious soldiers serving in the army (ultra-Orthodox soldiers do not undergo compulsory military service) to refuse to serve in units that allow females. Ultra-religious parties also demanded a law exempting Israeli Torah students from military service. The military considers such views dangerous for the Israel Defense Forces and the country, which depends on the coordinated and professional work of its military structures. If the authorities refuse to comply with the demands of ultra-religious parties, the latter will threaten to leave the coalition. That will lead to the collapse of the coalition and the election of a new government.

Netanyahu fired Israeli Defense Minister I. Galant. The country has been swept by a new wave of protests against laws changing the secular nature of democratic Israel. Netanyahu returned Galant to the post of defense minister.

Israel's enemies chose a problematic time for the country and attacked.

Islam

In 622, the Muslim prophet Muhammad appeared in Medina. He confiscated all lands belonging to tribes professing Judaism. His successor, Caliph Umar ibn Khattab, ordered all Jews to leave the central and northern regions of the Arabian Peninsula in the 640s. In 638, Jerusalem was captured by the warriors of Islam. This city became the third holiest place for Muslims after Mecca and Medina. In the 7th century, Arab troops conquered the countries of the Mediterranean and Europe. Conflict between Christians and Muslims was inevitable. This conflict continues today. Islam is the second-largest religion in the world.

In 1095, Pope Urban II proclaimed the First Crusade. The goal of the campaign was to liberate Jerusalem from Muslim rule. The First Crusade began with the massacre of European Jews. The illiterate peasants had no idea where Jerusalem was. But the infidel Jews were nearby and defenseless. The local population willingly supported pogroms and murders of Jews.

With the year 1099 came a new—and successful—crusade, and Jerusalem was captured on July 15. Of course, all this was accompanied by rivers of blood and brutal violence.

In 1187, the Sultan of Egypt and Syria, Salah ad-Din, defeated the Crusaders and recaptured Jerusalem.

* * *

The Ottoman Turks created the Ottoman state in northwest Asia in 1299. Islamized warlike descendants of Turkic nomadic pastoral tribes from Asia set out to conquer Europe. The Ottoman state, led by Sultan Mehmed II, conquered Constantinople in 1453, making the city its capital and renaming it Istanbul. During the reign of Sultan Selim (1512-1520), the Ottoman state became a caliphate. The conquests of the Ottoman Empire continued from the 6th century and extended from Anatolia to southeast Europe, western Asia, North Africa, Syria, Jordan, and Arabia. The Ottoman Empire ruled from 1517 to 1917. The First World War ended with the defeat of the Ottoman Empire.

* * **

The Middle East, contrary to the desire of the Arabs, who wanted to create a single Arab state, was divided between colonial states. Palestine and Mesopotamia in 1922 were controlled by the British Crown under a mandate issued by the League of Nations. The decision of the League of Nations proclaimed the implementation of the Balfour Declaration and the creation of a "Jewish national home" in Palestine.

Jews all over the world dreamed of returning to the lands of their ancestors. The first large-scale immigration (Jews call the return to the land of their ancestors' aliyah, i.e., repatriation) can be considered the exodus of Jews from Russia from 1882 to 1903.

* * *

The State of Israel was proclaimed on May 14, 1948, on the territory of the former Mandatory Palestine. This area has historical significance for Jews even before the Christian era. In three millennia BC, this area was inhabited by Canaanite tribes. In the 13th century BC, warlike tribes (sea peoples) from the islands of the Mediterranean Sea tried to invade Egypt and the southern territories of the Mediterranean coast. They captured the territory that is today called Gaza.

In the 9th century BC, ancient Jewish tribes founded the kingdom of Israel in the territories of Canaan, which subsequently split into two states—the kingdom of Israel in the north and the kingdom of Judah in the south. Between the Jews and the "peoples of the sea," whom the Jews called Plishtim, i.e., Philistines, there were wars for the possession of territories.

* * *

The Persians conquered the Babylonian kingdom in 538 BC. King Cyrus the Great led the conquest. The latter allowed all captive peoples to return to their territories, and the kingdom of Judah was restored.

The Persian state fell after a battle in 334 BC. All of Asia Minor came under the rule of Alexander the Great. After the commander's death, the conquered territories passed to his heirs and commanders. The kingdom of Judah came under Seleucid rule. The Jews continually rebelled against the Seleucid kingdom (166–142 BC), ending with the independence of Judea.

A new player on the world stage at the time, Rome, invaded the Middle East. The Jews rebelled against their new enslavers. The Jewish Wars against Roman rule, so-called by Josephus, continued unabated.

The Jews were expelled from their country by the Romans in 139 after the suppression of the Bar Kokhba revolt. Palestine is associated with the Philistine people who once lived on this land. Scattered among numerous nations, the Jews laid the foundation of a "diaspora" (a religious-ethnic group living in new places as a national-cultural minority) outside Judea.

* * *

Under Emperor Constantine the Great in 313, the Christian Church received the right to free activity in the Roman Empire. In the fourth century, the Roman Empire was divided into the Western (Catholic) and Eastern (Orthodox). Even though Christianity and the Christian faith are based on the teachings of the Jewish sect, which believed that the Messiah had already come in the form of Christ, it was not accepted by the bulk of the Jewish people.

Expelled from their country, the Jewish people scattered across numerous countries and continents known at that time.

For two long millennia, Jews wandered from country to country, sometimes remaining in a country for several centuries. Still, they were expelled again as strangers who did not want to accept the faith of whatever country they found shelter in. Jews scattered throughout the countries of Europe, the East, and Asia were subjected to persecution, pogroms, and murders.

* * *

During 711-718, Islamized North African Berber tribes invaded the Iberian Peninsula. The Visigoth army was defeated.

The conquered population was subject to tax (jizya), and the rebels were subjected to severe repression. There is information about those crucified in Cordoba, hanged in Granada, and beheaded in Toledo, Barcelona, and Seville. Mutamid ordered the beheadings in Seville: he decorated his palace with the severed heads of Jews and Christians. At Zamora, the heads were cut off on the orders of Al-Mansur, the vizier known as "the patron of philosophers and the greatest leader of Islamic Spain."

The Islamic state of Al-Andalus was formed on the conquered territory in Iberia, which existed until 1492.

The first Jewish settlements appeared in Spain (Sfarad, Hebrew) in 1000 BC. The mass migration of Jews to Spain occurred after the Romans expelled them from their land.

The conquest of the Iberian Peninsula began in the year of 711. At first, the conquerors used the knowledge of the Jews in various fields. During this period, Sephardic Jews held high positions. But very soon, the tolerant attitude gave way to repression.

The Jews moved north into areas conquered from the Arabs by the Spaniards. Christian kings were more tolerant of Sephardim. In 1492, the Spaniards defeated the Arabs. King Ferdinand and Queen Isabella gave Sephardim and Muslims the right to choose whether to be baptized or leave the country. Some Jewish families converted to Christianity and remained in Spain. The Spanish Inquisition kept a vigilant eye on converts (Maranos), and, at the slightest suspicion from the secret service about secret worship of the former faith, they subjected the Maranos to torture and punishment.

The expelled Jews settled in Western and Eastern Europe—and Muslim countries in Africa and the Middle East.

* * *

In the 9th century, Turks occupied vast territories of Asia as bearers of nomadic culture. The leader of one of the tribes, Osman, took the title "Sultan" in 1299, and his subjects began to be called Ottoman Turks.

In May 1453, the troops of Sultan Mehmed II attacked Constantinople. The fall of the Eastern Roman Empire, Byzantium, meant the end of a thousand years of the greatest empire in the world. The atrocities that marked the relationship between the conquerors and the civilian population were marked by the burning of abbeys, monasteries, desecration of churches, and the rape of nuns, Christians, and Jewish women, many of whom were sold into slavery or sent to harems.

By 1487, the Ottomans had subjugated all the Muslim possessions of the Asia Minor Peninsula. The name "Ottomans" became more prestigious than "Turks," and gradually, all Muslims of the Ottoman Empire (and not only Turkic-speaking ones), as well as Christians who converted to Islam in the Ottoman Empire, began to call themselves Ottomans. The warlike Ottomans conquered many territories: the Caucasus, Crimea, most of the Arabian Peninsula, the Balkan Peninsula, Egypt, North African countries, and many countries in Eastern Europe.

Jewish communities in Asia Minor existed long before the arrival of the Ottoman Turks. Jews expelled from Spain settled in many Muslim countries in the Middle East and Asia. Ottoman Sultan Bayezid II allowed exiled Jews from Spain and Portugal to settle in the Ottoman Empire.

* * *

The Jewish people lived in dispersion for more than 2,000 years. Jews were strangers everywhere; these people were considered guilty of the death of the Christian God and, according to Christian authorities, had to endure suffering and persecution. For all these centuries, Jews were brutally oppressed and persecuted. The persecution of Jews was especially severe in Christian Europe. From Spain in the west of Europe to Russia in the east, Jews living in Christian states were subjected to severe persecution, accused of various crimes, persecuted, and murdered. The Holocaust, the systematic mass extermination of Jews as directed by Nazi Germany's leader, Adolf Hitler, had reached its climax. For the "final solution to the Jewish question," Nazi Germany created extermination camps in which six million Jews were murdered.

Lord Arthur James Balfour played a crucial role in the history of the creation of the State of Israel. His name is closely associated with the so-called Balfour Declaration, formulated in November 1917. That was a letter sent by Lord Balfour, then British Foreign Secretary, to the leader of the British Jewish community, Lord Rothschild.

In this letter, the government expressed support for the creation of a "national home of the Jewish people" in Palestine, which was then under the control of the Ottoman Empire and subsequently came under the British Mandate. It is important to note that the declaration also emphasizes that nothing should be done to infringe on the civil and religious rights of existing non-Jewish communities in Palestine.

This declaration played a vital role in the further development of the Zionist movement and formed the basis of international support for the idea of the creation of Israel. Although issues related to the balance of interests between the Jewish and Arab populations of Palestine continued to be the subject of much debate and conflict, the Balfour Declaration significantly impacted the region's political landscape in the long term.

Hamas

The Islamic Resistance Movement called Hamas is a Palestinian Islamist movement founded in 1987. The political party Hamas "won" the Palestinian Legislative Council elections in the Gaza Strip in 2006, following the erroneous decision of the Israeli authorities to completely withdraw from the Gaza Strip. Hamas rejected the 1993 Oslo Peace Accords and declared a violent struggle against Israel to establish an Islamic state throughout Israel. Having taken control of the Gaza Strip, Hamas began to carry out attacks on both the military and the civilian population of Israel. They launched attacks on Israeli territory using Qassam's unguided missiles. Constant conflicts have led to an economic blockade of the Gaza Strip. In many countries, Hamas is recognized as a terrorist organization, except in Russia, Turkey, China, Qatar, and some other countries. Hamas is banned in Egypt and Jordan.

The Hamas attack on Israel on October 7, 2023, was the bloodiest attack on Israel in the last fifty years. As of October 13, 2023, Israeli losses were 1,200 dead and more than 3,500 wounded, and Hamas militants took more than 200 hostages (children, women, older adults). The amount of Israeli dead, wounded, and captured continues. The Israeli government declared martial law in the country and launched a military operation against the Gaza Strip.

The dead were buried throughout the country. The names of those responsible for the terrible destruction and loss of life will become known after the investigation. Israel has never known such a catastrophic tragedy. The hostages must be released. This priority task was assigned to the army.

The hostage-taking terrorists followed the example of Iran. In 1979, during the Carter administration in the U.S., the American embassy in Iran, with the 66 diplomats working there, was seized by an overexcited crowd that turned violent. Iran's new revolutionary government approved the taking of hostages. The American government sent a group of specialist saboteurs, Delta Force, to forcibly free the hostages. To America's great embarrassment, the mission failed. Negotiations continued until 1981, when the hostages were released.

The Hamas movement is based on the Egyptian Muslim Brotherhood and the Palestinian Islamic Jihad. Israel allowed Hamas to receive donations from Gulf countries. Hamas has enjoyed the support of Israel, which views Hamas as a competitor in the fight against the PLO (Palestine Liberation Organization). Hamas received assistance from the Soviet Union, Qatar, Iran, and other Muslim countries. The withdrawal of Israeli troops from the Gaza Strip in 2005 contributed to the popularity of Hamas.

Russian President Vladimir Putin invited a Hamas delegation to visit Moscow. Friendship agreements were signed. Today, we know that it was Russia that provided Hamas with information about Israel's military situation as of October 7, 2024. Iran was behind this entire operation, and China financed everything.

The Hamas program provides for the destruction of the State of Israel and its replacement with an Islamic theocratic (secular and spiritual power in one person) republic.

In 2007, Israel declared the Gaza Strip a "hostile entity" and began an economic blockade. The constant escalation of conflicts led to a large-scale military operation in the Gaza Strip called Cast Lead. The UN has harshly criticized Israel.

Hamas founder Ahmed Yassin said: "Any Jew can be considered a military settler, and we must kill him."

> *Hamas is not so much anti-Israel as a religious Islamist anti-Semitic organization, and its goal is to build an Islamist state in the Gaza Strip, which does not need peace with Israel.*
> – Frank Staunton, University of London

Hamas' goals, tactics, methods of attack, and inhuman cruelty resemble those of ISIS. The prevalence of Hamas in Israel, Syria, Lebanon, and other Islamic states is reminiscent of ISIS tactics. The destruction of Hamas militants in Israel does not mean a final victory over this terrorist Islamist organization. The many-headed hydra of hatred and thirst for revenge will arise again and again.

Hamas and Hezbollah are essentially Iran's proxies for certain missions. The entry of Hezbollah into the war in northern Israel will mean the opening of a second front and another ground operation in Lebanon. The United States has warned Hezbollah against entering the conflict between Israel and Hamas.

Another war in the Middle East has become a reality. The interests of many countries intertwine in this unstable region. Iran supports most radical Islamist regimes. Russia needs Iran's drones because it is bogged down in a war against Ukraine and needs the weapons that Iran supplies. Various Islamic states support the Palestinians. In Lebanon, a vast Hezbollah army, another proxy for Iran, is preparing to attack Israel from the north. The Houthis in the southern Arabian Peninsula have officially declared war on Israel. Turkish President Tayyip Erdogan said: "We will declare Israel a war criminal." There is the possibility of intervention in a military conflict in the Middle East: Russia, Iran, Turkey, China, the Gulf countries, the United States, and their allies. A local conflict can develop into a regional one, followed by World War III. Nobody wants this except radical regimes. If this does happen, no one will need popcorn.

Hamas rejected the 1993 Oslo Peace Accords and declared a violent struggle against Israel to establish an Islamic state throughout Israel. They launched attacks on Israeli territory using unguided Qassam missiles.

The Israeli government declared martial law and launched a military operation against the Gaza Strip. The names of those responsible for the terrible destruction and loss of life will become known after the investigation. Israel has never known such a catastrophic tragedy. The hostages must be released. This priority task was assigned to the army.

* * *

Hezbollah—the Party of Allah—is a paramilitary Lebanese Shiite organization seeking to create an Islamic Shiite state. They have practically seized power in Lebanon. The leader of this party, Hassan Nasrallah, does not exclude Hezbollah's participation in the armed conflict between Israel and Hamas. The United States and other Western countries have designated Hezbollah as a terrorist organization. Israel fought twice against Hezbollah in Lebanon.

Why are Israelis and Palestinians fighting? The roots of this hatred and confrontation can be traced to ancient times. The Jews were expelled from their country by the Romans in 139 after numerous Jewish wars and the Bar Kokhba revolt. Emperor Hadrian ordered the destruction of Jerusalem. Following Roman traditions, the land was plowed with oxen and sprinkled with salt. On the site of Jerusalem, the pagan city of Aelia Capitolina was founded. The very name of the country—Judea—was replaced by "Palestine." This name is associated with the Philistine people who once lived on this land. The Bible mentions these people and their confrontation with the second Jewish king, David. The Jewish people were expelled from their country and dispersed across numerous countries and continents known at the time. For two long millennia, Jews wandered from country to country, sometimes settling for several centuries but then being expelled as strangers who did not want to accept the faith of the country in which they found refuge. Jews scattered throughout the countries of Europe, the East, and Asia were subjected to persecution, pogroms, and murders.

Under Emperor Constantine the Great in 313, the Christian Church received the right to free activity in the Roman Empire.

In the fourth century, the Roman Empire was divided into the Western (Catholic) and Eastern (Orthodox). Even though the basis of the Christian faith is Judaism, all twelve apostles and the Christian Lord Jesus Christ himself were Jews, and the Torah (Old Testament) is included in the Bible; from the first days of its existence, Christianity accused the Jews of the death of Christ, thus putting the very beginning of the persecution of Jews.

For Hamas, this is a holy religious war against the Jewish people who professed Judaism. Hamas does not recognize Israel's right to exist.

Hamas is a religious terrorist organization. This organization is Iran's proxy (trusted group, authorized entity). Hamas sponsors include Iran, Qatar, and Turkey, as well as private sponsors living in the Gulf countries and Palestinians living in Europe and the United States. Hamas has purchased the most modern weapons they could afford to arm the militants. Hamas fighters are trained inside the enclave in Syria and Iran. Israel believes that there are ten thousand missiles of varying ranges up to 200 km in the Gaza Strip. For the Palestinians the end goal is to destroy all Jews. At the very least, they call for the expulsion of all Jews from this land. The mythology of this land lies at the heart of the conflict between Jews and Muslims. There has been a certain amount of enmity among followers of the three religions, Judaism, Christianity, and Islam since time immemorial. The territory of modern Israel is considered a holy land for all three religions. The center of this land is Jerusalem.

For Jews, this is the land where God began to create the world. The First Temple (of Solomon) was built here, but the Babylonians destroyed it under the leadership of

Nebuchadnezzar. The second temple at the destruction site was restored by Jews returning from Babylonian captivity under the leadership of the priest Ezra. The Jewish king Herod the Great rebuilt the temple in all its splendor, but the Romans destroyed it. The remaining part of the wall is the Western Wall, the most essential Jewish shrine.

For Christians, Jerusalem is the holy city in which Christ was crucified, and from here, he ascended to heaven after his resurrection. The Church of the Holy Sepulchre, the main shrine of Christians, was built here.

For Muslims, Jerusalem is a holy place from where the Prophet Muhammad ascended to meet Allah. The Al-Aqsa Mosque was built on the Temple Mount to honor this event. That is the third most crucial Muslim shrine after Mecca and Medina.

The mythology of religions passed down through millennia explains the implacable hostility between Israelis and Palestinians. This intractable problem has no solution in the modern history of our species.

The Qur'an contains forty-three verses referencing Bani Yisrael (Children of Israel). The Arabic term for Jews is Yahudi. Muhammad invited the Jews to convert to Islam, explaining that he was a prophet sent by God, according to the Jewish scriptures. The Jews refused, showering Muhammad with ridicule. That was taken as a declaration of war. Hadiths (sayings of the Prophet Muhammad): "The Day of Judgment will not come until the Muslims, fighting with the Jews, ensure that the Jews hide behind stones and trees. The stones and trees will tell them: "O Muslims, O Abdullah, there is a Jew behind me, come and kill him."

Maimonides and his assessment of the attitude of Muslims toward Jews:

"...As a punishment for our sins, God has thrown us to the mercy of this people, the people of Ishmael (that is, Muslims), who persistently persecute us, develop ways to harm us and ways to humiliate us. No nation has ever done more harm to Israel. Nobody wanted to humiliate Jews like that. No one could humiliate us like they did... We endured their desire for our violent humiliation, their lies, their absurdities that go beyond human capabilities... Despite this, we are not spared from their ferocity and evil at any time. On the contrary, the more we suffer and try to give in to them, the more militant and aggressive they become towards us."

Hamas confirmed its intention to fight the existence of Israel:

"The whole land from the Jordan River in the east to the Mediterranean Sea on the west should belong to Muslims."

* * *

And so another day of Israel's war with Hamas terrorists continues. The army entered the enclave territory and continued to clear the territory cautiously, realizing the complexity of the tasks facing the troops. Hamas, thanks to Iran, Russia, Turkey, Qatar, and other Israel-hating guardians, is equipped with the most modern military-technical means to wage war with Israel and has been digging underground tunnels and shelters for many years. According to numerous data collected by Israeli intelligence, the length of the tunnel network could be 500 to 700 km. Those tunnels housed factories to produce missiles, mines, and bombs. This underground complex poses a significant challenge as some sections of the tunnels can be as deep as 70 meters underground. Besides the danger of traps and the difficulty of navigating such a labyrinth, experts believe that this is where most of the hostages captured by Hamas in the early days of the war are located. The tunnels are probably mined, and any attempt at fighting there would be very problematic. Israel uses robots and trained dogs. The main problem remains the priority task of rescuing the hostages. Due to the difficulty of waging a tunnel war and the reluctance to risk soldiers' lives, the command believes the war could last several months.

In the north of the country, in Lebanon, there is another even bigger and better armed Hezbollah group, much more dangerous and equipped by Iran with missiles and modern weapons. Hezbollah has practically seized power in Lebanon. The Lebanese economy has been destroyed, Israel's northern border is unresolved, and constant clashes occur. Israel keeps the Northern Group of Forces there at the ready.

There is no doubt that Israel will win the confrontation with Hamas, perhaps even among the leaders of Hamas, many of whom have already been liquidated.

Israel's goals:
A) Destroy Hamas, as an organization whose main goal is to destroy the state of Israel.
B) Release hostages forcibly held in the Gaza Strip.
C) The question that occupies the minds of many people today is what will happen to the people living in Gaza and what to do with the territory itself. The fact that this

territory cannot be given into the hands of terrorists is not even discussed. That has already happened once. It was a political failure of the government; in August 2005, following the Oslo Accords (1993), signed between Israel and the PLO (Palestine Liberation Organization), Israel withdrew its troops from the Gaza Strip and liquidated Jewish settlements.

The Islamist organization Hamas seized power in the Gaza Strip in October 2006, and it was then that the militarization of the Gaza Strip began. As of 2023, the population of the Gaza Strip was over two million. The status of the Gaza Strip after the end of the war remains open.

UN chief Antonio Guterres has called for an immediate humanitarian ceasefire in the Middle East to ease "human suffering of epic proportions" caused by the conflict between Israel and the Gaza Strip. For Antonio Guterres, this is a conflict, not a war, between civilization and the fanatical savages of the twenty-first century, ready to destroy everything including the people living in the Gaza Strip. Hamas is ready to take to the grave everything that does not correspond to its ideas about the goal: "The liberation of all Palestine from the river (Jordan) to the sea (Mediterranean) is our strategic goal, and there is no goal more sacred and important. "

* * *

Hamas fighters are ready to sacrifice their lives in the name of Allah in exchange for a reward in the next world that goes to martyrs. The countless sweet, innocent кhuri and heavenly bliss, to them, are worth dying for.

While the weary martyrs enjoy the delights of paradise, the Israelis will have to decide what to do next with all this territory and a population that could reach two million people. Everything is destroyed in Gaza. The economy is obliterated. Everything needs to be restored, starting with clearing the rubble and burying the corpses. Everything is necessary. Money solves many problems; the international community will help ameliorate living conditions in the devastated Gaza Strip.

However, the central question of what to do next with the problematic Gaza Strip remains open. Israel has no right to leave this sector without proper control to avoid repeating the mistake of withdrawing troops in the hope that everything will work out. The resurgence of Hamas, Islamic Jihad, or any other religious Islamist group is unacceptable.

Without a doubt, this issue is being discussed in the government, in the press, and on social networks. On Channel 9 of Israeli television, one of the guests expressed an idea that may be worthy of everyone's attention. The essence of this proposal is that the Gaza Strip could host a US naval base. Millions of Palestinians in the Gaza Strip will find good jobs that will provide them with a decent life. A substantial naval base will allow the United States to oversee the security of countries in the Middle East: Egypt, Turkey, Syria, Lebanon, Jordan, countries of the African continent, the Mediterranean, and the Arabian Peninsula. This presence will benefit Saudi Arabia, Egypt, Jordan, and many other countries. Russia's influence in this region will decrease significantly.

Even more dangerous than the Hamas militants on the militarized Gaza Strip, is the paramilitary Shiite group Hezbollah in southern Lebanon, which is also closely linked, like Hamas, to the fanatical jihadist regime of the Shiite ayatollahs in Iran. Hezbollah has the largest non-state army in the world. The leader of the Shiite radical group, Hassan Nasrallah, has been hiding in a bunker for twenty years, recording his speeches, which are distributed by the media. Israel fought wars with Lebanon in 1982 and 2006. The IDF maintains significant forces on its northern borders, ready at any moment to repel an attack by Hezbollah militants. A war on two fronts will significantly complicate Israel's situation, but the country's military-political leadership expects victory.

* * *

The United States has sent naval forces, air defense systems, and military personnel to the Middle East. The Near and Middle East region is more important today than ever. The increased importance of hydrocarbons, which this region is rich in, contributes to the energy security of many countries worldwide, influencing world politics. The constant threat of the Arab-Israeli conflict and the threat of nuclear proliferation require close attention and the ability to neutralize this threat. Following the adoption of the Eisenhower Doctrine in 1957, the US National Security Strategy began including the Middle East region.

Before the start of the war between Hamas and Israel, the White House conducted intensive negotiations in the Near and Middle East on the creation of an economic corridor:

India-UAE-Middle East-Saudi Arabia-Jordan-Israel-Europe. This corridor was supposed to counteract the expansion of China's "Silk Path." The US initiative included huge investments in shipping, rail, internet cables, and more that would bring stability and prosperity to the Middle East. Today, these negotiations are at a standstill. To establish lasting peace in the Middle East after the end of the war, Saudi Arabia may take de jure control of Gaza. If this happens, everyone will benefit, and peace can reign in the Middle East.

* * *

On the 41st day of the war, Israeli IDF troops occupied the northern part of the Gaza Strip. The bulk of the northern residents of the strip were temporarily evacuated to the southern part of Gaza. These measures were taken to minimize civilian deaths. Leaflets were dropped from the air throughout the region, and the civilian population in the southern Gaza Strip was notified in no uncertain terms, through loudspeakers in Arabic, that they needed to leave. The Israeli command announced hours-long humanitarian breaks and guarded corridors for free movement south of the sector. Neither Egypt, Jordan, nor any other Muslim state agreed to accept those fleeing the Gaza Strip, even temporarily. They know very well what Hamas is and what will happen if they allow this group to establish itself in their country.

The Israeli military moved very slowly and carefully into the Gaza Strip. The IDF command was afraid of harming the hostages taken by Hamas on 10/07/2023. Hamas has created its own military communications, weapons workshops, warehouses, rocket launchers, command posts, etc. In the so-called Gaza metro, which extends underground to a considerable depth and has a length of more than 500 kilometers, the Israeli command is trying to protect its military from booby traps and other surprises in the multi-story labyrinth of the Gaza metro.

Without recognizing Israel's right to exist, Hamas was conceived by its spiritual leader, Sheikh Ahmed Yassin. He was a member of the political-religious organization "Muslim Brotherhood" and banned in many states as a terrorist. Yassin was killed in the Gaza Strip in 2004. Hamas has constantly opposed Israel. Rocket attacks, kidnappings, bombings, and provocations on the Israeli border have led to the deaths of many Israelis.

The forty-sixth day of the war has arrived, Israel fighting against the Hamas terrorists. The northern part of the Gaza Strip and Gaza City itself are under the control of Israeli IDF troops. Stockpiles of weapons, missiles, and explosives were found in hospitals, kindergartens, schools, playgrounds, and public buildings. All this served as a cover for Hamas militants and its leaders.

Most of the population of Gaza City was evacuated to the south of the strip to avoid numerous casualties in the war waged by Hamas.

IDF soldiers are opening more and more underground concrete tunnels and at greater depths. That is no longer the "Gaza metro"; it is a vast underground city with tunnels dug in all directions, including under the concrete wall between Israel and the Gaza Strip. This concrete monolithic wall was twenty meters deep and was equipped with sensors in case anyone approached it. Why none of these precautionary measures worked, and why the Hamas militants were able to simply demolish the fence on the surface in several places, remains to be investigated after the end of the war. There were so many mistakes that future political and military miscalculation trials should be made public, and those responsible should receive the punishment they deserve.

During the Yom Kippur War in 1973, when Egyptian and Syrian troops attacked Israel, the country was unprepared for this war. Israel won, but ongoing investigations into government failures led to Golda Meir's resignation. That was an Israeli intelligence failure fifty years ago. Today, this shame has repeated itself. Then, Golda Meir's government resigned. Today, we see arrogance, ignorance, and an insatiable thirst to lead the country among the authorities, which has led to disastrous consequences. The war continues, and today, we still do not know how many victims the Israeli people will have to mourn before hostilities end.

Was Hamas counting on chaos in the Netanyahu government? The world has probably seen numerous demonstrations of protest against the government and its unfounded decisions. If Hamas itself did not understand what was happening, then its "mentors and well-wishers" pushed the terrorists, hoping with the help of Hamas to inflict a crushing defeat on Israel. The names of these "mentors and well-wishers" must be revealed after Israel's victory.

A temporary truce, or rather a temporary suspension of hostilities between Israel and Hamas, which not only Israel's allies but also the entire international "liberal" community insisted on, may take place. The suffering of the Palestinian "civilian" population in the Gaza Strip was reported by the media, representatives of various countries speaking from the UN rostrum, and numerous fans of the "unfortunate" Palestinians around the world. Television showed the horrific suffering of the "civilian population" of Gaza, suffering due to the fault of the Israeli military. Of course, Hamas was condemned for kidnapping Jewish children, older adults, and women. However, the IDF's "disproportionate" response to Israel was widely condemned. As the satirist Mikhail Zhvanetsky said: "Guys, you have to be more careful."

Being "friendly" toward Jews is nothing new for Israelis. During more than two thousand years of dispersion among other peoples, the Jews went through torment, suffering, extermination, contempt, genocide, and its culmination—the extermination of six million Jews in Nazi Germany, the Holocaust.

Hamas requested a temporary truce in exchange for hostages. It is clear that "not all for all," but many, many Palestinians sitting in Israeli prisons, a small number of Israeli hostages. Negotiations took place in Qatar. Israel does not negotiate directly with terrorists, and Qatar has acted as a mediator. Hamas, convinced of the softness of the Israelis, asked for a lot. They asked for a break in hostilities, supplying Gaza with fuel, food, water, medicine, and other "humanitarian" items necessary for the war economy. The preliminary agreement specified a ratio of one to three. For every Israeli hostage, Hamas receives three Palestinian prisoners.

Israel releases Palestinian women and children, "juvenile criminals," that is, frees 150 Palestinian women and teenagers and others who do not have "Jewish blood on their hands." Israel detains fifty women and children. A four-day break in hostilities was to come into force on Thursday, November 23, 2023. But something didn't work. Attempt number two is due to take place on Friday, January 24, 2023. Hamas says many of the hostages are being held by various independent militant groups hoping to profit from "human trafficking." But Hamas itself does not even know who is holding these unfortunates, where and in what conditions they are being kept, and whether they are alive.

These people lived in another millennium when the capture of women and children gave good baksheesh (earnings from blood). One can only hope that the rest who believe in God can pray.

On Friday evening of November 2024 at 16:00, an exchange of Israeli hostages for Palestinian prisoners held in Israeli prisons for various crimes is scheduled. Israel cannot do otherwise. In this country, the life of the country's citizens is sacred. In all likelihood, if Hamas could, it would not hesitate to sacrifice the lives of all its fellow tribe members for the destruction of the hated Israelis. By exposing these unfortunate people to the fires of war and death, Hamas proved how little the people of Palestine mean to them. No Arab country wanted to shelter, at least during the war, two million Palestinian refugees. Jordan, Egypt, and Lebanon know firsthand from bitter experience what the displacement of "Palestinian civilians" entails.

Israel is waiting for the return of its hostages, children, women, and elderly people. Qatar, Egypt, and the United States were guaranteed the deal. Hamas is triumphant—they became the heroes of the day. The whole world is talking and watching what Hamas is doing. The leaders of many countries vouched for that. Disgusting terrorists who kill and kidnap children, women, and the elderly are now triumfators. They were killing anyone who could be shot, stabbed, or burned alive. Wild animals kill their victims when they are hungry; Hamas kills its victims whenever possible when they know they won't encountering resistance. The bloody orgy of unpunished murders and the tears and suffering of the unfortunate victims evoke a feeling of permissiveness and only instills Hamas with more courage to perpetrate these deeds.

But today, there is a desperate desire to live and escape at any cost. The hostages were taken precisely on this day. Today, you can bargain, present different conditions, somehow maneuver, and try to stay alive. Retribution is at hand. It's unavoidable. The survivors will be judged. Justice will prevail. But evil is indestructible. The poisonous reptile of hatred and the desire to kill will raise its bloody head, thirsting for the fresh blood of the innocent. Who will be the next victim of the multi-headed hydra?

* * *

On October 24, 2023, at 4:00 p.m., after a long wait and much excitement, all of Israel witnessed, with a sigh of relief, thirteen hostages being brought back into the country. They were saved and treated by doctors, psychologists, and people called upon to deal with the consequences of traumatic incidents. Relatives and friends were notified and waiting to hug their loved ones. That cannot be forgotten nor can it be forgiven. There were still three nail-biting days ahead of us, waiting for the release of the remaining 37 hostages. The agreement with the terrorists provides for the exchange of 50 Israelis for 150 Palestinians.

The fate of the remaining Israeli hostages held by Hamas is still unclear. The fact that terrorists cannot be trusted is clear to any Israeli. Hundreds, maybe thousands of people will work to ensure the transaction goes smoothly. Common sense dictates that when dealing with wild, unpredictable killers, you should expect the worst (most likely the worst). The possibility of a bloody bacchanalia is at the forefront of the world's attention when all the cameras are pointed at Hamas. Failure of a deal under any flimsy pretext. A desire to change the terms of the deal, a test of how far Israel will go to appease the terrorists and save its citizens.

On the evening of November February 5, 2024, at 16:00, another exchange of Israeli hostages for Palestinian prisoners held in Israeli prisons is scheduled.

Israel is waiting for its hostages, children, women, and elderly people.

The bloody orgies of Hamas, unpunished murders, tears, and suffering of the unfortunate victims are the essence of the Islamists' struggle.

The four-day ceasefire between Hamas and Israel, which Western media calls a truce, continued on Saturday, October 25. On the second day of the four agreed upon, the second stage of the release of Israeli hostages should take place. At 6:45 p.m., the Rafah checkpoint between Egypt and the Gaza Strip was crowded with cars with their lights flashing. Egypt said the hostage deal had taken place. The Red Cross, which is handling the deal, denied the report. Hamas said it stopped the hostage exchange due to insufficient humanitarian aid being delivered.

Then a second Hamas statement appeared: Israeli UAVs were circling over the territory of Southern Gaza, which for Hamas was a violation of the terms of the "truce." Egypt says the negotiations continue. Hamas leader: "This is propaganda." Israel rejected new claims by Hamas, which demanded that Hamas members, not women and children, be released from prisons for exchange.

Israel warned Hamas of resuming hostilities at 0.00 am on November 26, 2023, if the return of the hostages does not take place, as provided for in the temporary ceasefire agreement. Late in the evening of November 25, Hamas released the second batch of hostages.

The IDF reported 17 hostages: 13 Israelis and 4 Thais. All of them are already in Israel. There are still two agreed-upon days left before the return of the hostages. Whether a new temporary ceasefire agreement will be reached depends on Hamas. As of today, the Military Committee has decided to extend possible new deadlines for a temporary ceasefire, but in general, it will be by no more than ten days. The decision to destroy Hamas's political and military structure remains the top priority of the operation in the Gaza Strip.

On the third day of the ceasefire agreement, November 26, 2023, the exchange of Israeli hostages for Palestinian prisoners in Israeli prisons happened as agreed. The conditions were the same: for every Israeli, the terrorists demanded three Palestinians. Israel fulfilled the terms of the deal, and today, the whole world sees who Hamas is fighting with. Hamas claimed they only attacked Israeli soldiers, but during the hostage exchange, the world saw small children and older women being exchanged. The false propaganda of Hamas is clear to any unbiased person. The exchange took place at the agreed time and without any problems. Hamas released 17 hostages. Among them were 14 Israelis, one hostage with a Russian passport, and four-year-old Abigail Edan with dual American-Israeli citizenship; the rest were women and children.

The fourth and final day of the agreed exchange of hostages taken by Hamas terrorists for Palestinians held in Israeli prisons has arrived, but since the victims of the attack fortunately survived, these criminals are believed to have "no Jewish blood" on their hands

Israel received a list of 11 Israeli hostages who will be released on the last day of the ceasefire, November 27, 2023. On the list, some relatives of the released hostages remained in the hands of Hamas. Israel protested because this was contrary to the agreement. Pressure was mounting on Israel to extend the ceasefire and find a solution to the conflict between Israel and the Palestinians.

On the evening of November 27, 2023, the exchange of Israeli hostages for Palestinian criminals serving sentences in Israeli prisons took place with minor violations of the agreed protocol. On the same day, Israel received an offer to extend the ceasefire for two more days in exchange for 20 Israelis (10 per day) and 60 Palestinian prisoners (30 per day). Israel gave its consent to this deal.

On the afternoon of November 28, 2023, Israel received a list of 10 names of Israeli hostages. Previously, there were cases where the names of hostages were changed immediately before the exchange, which caused understandable anger and protest from Israel. Preparations for the fifth day of the exchange of Israeli hostages for Palestinian prisoners proceeded as usual.

Suddenly, a message appeared online about a new proposal from Hamas that Israel end military operations in the Gaza Strip; in response, Hamas would release all hostages, civilian and military. As is usually the case, there were many supporters and opponents of the proposed agreement.

Supporters advocated for an immediate end to the war since the main goal—

the return of the hostages—would be achieved. The prime minister who ends the war and returns all the hostages can expect to be re-elected.

Opponents of such an agreement noted that the main goal—the destruction of Hamas—would not succeed. A prime minister who signs such an agreement is doomed to shame and defeat. Sane people offered a simple solution: Hamas surrenders all its weapons and comes out with its hands raised, admitting defeat. An international tribunal was being created in Israel to try crimes committed by Hamas members and make sure the punishment fit the crime. Channel 9 on Israeli television offered Israeli citizens an open vote on the channel's website.

The next day of the ceasefire between Israel and Hamas, November 29, 2023, was spent not only in anticipation of the ten hostages taken on October 7, 2023, but also in heated debates on the internet and television about Hamas's proposals. The apparent pressure on the Israeli leadership from the "progressive public," not excluding the United States, was increasing with the demand to end the war and find a peaceful solution to the Palestinian problem. Israel has become bound to its policy of releasing Israeli citizens captured by Hamas; that was what Hamas was counting on. After the apparent reluctance of Hezbollah and

Iran to participate in hostilities (i.e., come to the aid of Hamas), the latter can count on pressure from its supporters in Europe, the USA, and elsewhere. Israel cannot refuse to live in anticipation of the exchange of its hostages for Palestinian prisoners and also cannot refuse the final defeat of Hamas. Otherwise, it risks stepping on the same rake. As the famous Roman senator Cato the Elder ended his speeches, "and Carthage must be destroyed," the wartime Israeli government declares, "Hamas must be destroyed."

Relatives of the hostages demand peace with Hamas. In this case, shame is guaranteed for any government that gives in to such demands, followed by mass resignations and, possibly, the trial of the government in power. The decision must be made immediately. Time is working against the State of Israel. Another group of Israeli hostages was handed over to the Egyptian Red Cross. That is an agreed procedure—Hamas hands over the hostages to the Red Cross, which hands over the hostages to the Israelis.

What will the wartime government decide? What will the extended meeting of the Israeli government decide?

Late in the evening of November 29, 2023, another exchange of Israeli hostages for Palestinian prisoners finally took place. Israel received not 10 but 12 hostages. Hamas explained its generosity by thanking Russian President Vladimir Putin for his courageous defense of Hamas. Two hostages had dual citizenship: Israeli and Russian.

Another ceasefire was declared before more exchanges of Israeli hostages for Palestinian prisoners took place. Hamas decided not to be generous and sent a list of eight names, citing the previous day when two hostages were added. Israel swallowed this "slap in the face," according to the principle of "take what they give." No one can confidently say how long this cat-and-mouse game will continue. It can be assumed that the wartime government will accept the imposed ceasefire rules in exchange for Israeli hostages and wait for Hamas to make a mistake and violate the ceasefire terms. US President Joe Biden advocates for a permanent ceasefire, increased humanitarian aid to Gazans, punishment of Hamas, and the creation of two states for two peoples. The fact that these concepts are incompatible does not occur to him and his assistants. And if it happens, then Israel must say what the world community wants to hear. Biden has an election on the horizon and does not want to part with the prestigious position of US president. Biden's enemies are not asleep and are preparing a very unpleasant "surprise" for him: an analysis of the activities of the Biden family, corruption schemes, and the participation of Biden family members in many transactions.

"In every home has its playful ears," and Israel has its problems and upcoming trials, reminiscent of the well-known and eternal Russian question: "Who is to blame? What to do?"

* * *

As of December 1, 2023, Hamas offered to exchange 10 Israelis (7 women and three corpses) for 30 Palestinian prisoners serving in Israeli prisons for various crimes. Israel refused the deal: "First, we want to get all the living hostages, and then the bodies of the dead." In response to this proposal, Hamas violated the ceasefire, and early in the morning, an air raid siren sounded in and around Sderot. In war, as in war. The Israeli army attacked Hamas targets along the entire front.

Political scientists and military analysts expressed their thoughts on Hamas's behavior in this situation. The most likely version: Hamas could not collect the required number of living hostages.

Islamic Jihad and smaller terrorist groups are unwilling to share captured hostages with Hamas. In such a situation, it's every man for himself. You can negotiate benefits for yourself in exchange for hostages: life, money, and possible freedoms.

Qatar continues negotiations with Hamas to convince the latter to agree to the ceasefire and make concessions. Israel continues to attack Hamas throughout Gaza. Nobody knows whether there will be another ceasefire. Will Hamas stop resisting and raise its hands in surrender? This would not be enough. Hamas and its fellow terrorists must hand over all living Israeli hostages and then all the bodies of the dead so that their families can bury them according to Jewish customs.

Baruch Dayan Chaemet ברוך דיין חמת

* * *

On December 2, 2023, the temporary ceasefire between Israel and Hamas terrorists has already been forgotten, but again, explosions are heard along the entire front. Hamas, which has broken the fragile truce, is sending rockets into southern Israel. He, in turn, attacks the north, center, and south of the Gaza Strip. For Israel, the priority remains the destruction of Hamas's military and political control, the release of hostages, and the restoration of security in the attacked territories. For Hamas, the main goal is the destruction of the State of Israel and its population. In such a radical confrontation, the loser must disappear forever, not unlike how ISIS, Al-Qaida, the Islamic State, and other modern terrorists disappeared.

Israel is fighting on several fronts simultaneously. In addition to Hamas in the Gaza Strip, its militants terrorize Judea and Samaria, territories under the jurisdiction of the Palestinian Authority. There are Hamas militants in Lebanon, Syria, and Iraq. Hezbollah in southern Lebanon, which voluntarily maintained a ceasefire in solidarity with Hamas terrorists, has resumed shelling northern Israel. The Houthis, Iran's proxies, on the southern tip of the Arabian Peninsula, are firing missiles at Eilat and seizing merchant ships in the Red Sea, claiming they belong to the Israelis. Russia, China, and Iran are conducting joint naval exercises in the Gulf of Oman.

Israel will undergo profound changes after the end of the war: political, military, economic, and strategic. The world has changed radically. Russia in Europe, China in Asia, Iran in the Middle East: all these formidable confrontations in world politics require a new approach and new tactics in this unstable world. Nobody wants a Third World War except jihadists and other terrorists—especially nuclear wars. There will be no winners. If a global conflagration occurs, the survivors of the infected, poisoned world will ultimately perish from disease and hunger. The UN, a stillborn creation in the post-war world, cannot withstand the threats of our century. The United States, the main bastion of the democratic world, is torn by internal problems and an unprecedented influx of immigrants. Old liberal Europe is already filled with immigrants from the East and Africa.

There is nowhere to run today. It's easier for those who believe in the omnipotence of higher powers. They believe in helping when it is needed. Six million Jews believed in the afterlife and the help of the Almighty. The rest must try to save this unstable world.

> *Oh, war, what have you done, vile:*
> *Our courtyards have become quiet,*
> *Our boys raised their heads –*
> *They have matured before the time came*
> *Barely loomed on the threshold*
> *And they left, the soldier by the soldier...*
>
> – Bulat Okudzhava

Israel, surrounded by enemies, woke up from the intoxication of silence and euphoria. October 7, 2023, struck everyone precisely with its unexpectedness and apparent lack of preparation for the dangers of a new war. The country woke up to a different world. Where there are vile and insidious enemies, and you can't dance carefree on the border with your monster neighbor. Not all Israel's neighboring states suffer from the desire to become friendly and peaceful neighbors but want all the Jews to go back to their countries of origin or somewhere else. The years of seemingly peaceful silence, which allowed politicians to divide the big pie, the country's budget, according to the principles "you give something to me, I give something to you," are over.

Power is an intoxicating drug that, once tasted, can lead to long-term addiction. Power is a big casino with marked arts, where the winner gets everything except criminal liability.

Nobody expected war: not political rulers, senior military leadership, intelligence services, nor those responsible for military units' combat and mobilization readiness. Upon the first shots, jeeps with a duty team and a desire to restore order were sent to the border with the Gaza Strip. The soldiers came under fire from numerous well-armed enemies, ready for murder, and soldiers got killed. A new jeep with a new team was sent to check what was happening there. They ended up in the same meat grinder.

Police officers armed with pistols were killed on the spot, much like members of local self-defense units, who have one machine gun and maybe a couple of pistols. Several thousand heavily armed terrorists rushed in, spreading death and terror. The result of the first day's massacre was more than 1,200 killed in the first hours and more than 250 kidnapped. Someone must be responsible for this.

Three hundred sixty thousand reservists were drafted into the army. There was a lack of materials, military support, and uniforms. The population rushed to collect warm socks, underwear, food, and everything the soldiers might need in war.

Someone must be responsible for this, too.

War is war, but lunch is on schedule. Shoes for soldiers must be the correct size. Otherwise, the soldier will not operate at his best. Someone must be responsible for this, too.

Thanks to the soldiers and commanders of the Israeli army. They saved this country.

Thanks to the United States, which sent two flotillas and a nuclear submarine. That cooled those who wanted to "help" Hamas "finally resolve the Jewish question."

This war will end with the defeat of Hamas. Who is next?

* * *

Next up is Hezbollah in Lebanon. Israel fought Hezbollah in the Second Lebanon War in 2006. In 34 days of fighting, Israel lost 160 people killed. Under the terms of the truce agreement, Hezbollah was ordered to withdraw north of the Litany River, and the demarcation border occupied by five thousand peacekeepers and the Lebanese military. These conditions have been violated, and today Hezbollah is on the Lebanese border with Israel.

Hezbollah is a Shia group and Iranian proxy in the Middle East. The group's behavior ultimately depends on Shiite Iran, the sponsor of the Sunni Hamas. Religious differences do not matter in a war against a common enemy—Israel. On the border with Lebanon, where Hezbollah has occupied the south, Israel keeps a third of its army on alert. Israel's shelling does not stop, responding with artillery fire and airstrikes on Hezbollah positions, trying to suppress the points from which the firing was coming from. The situation is abnormal, but Israel is trying not to make it worse. Israel evacuated civilians in the north of the country, more than 10 km from the border with Lebanon. When asked whether Hezbollah would enter the war to support Hamas in its confrontation with Israel, military experts offered differing opinions. Hamas leaders feel abandoned and demand more decisive action. Hezbollah said that when Israel crosses the "red line," they will enter into conflict. Of course, Iran makes the decision. The Lebanese authorities oppose any military action. The Shiite group, which has practically seized power in Lebanon, is waiting for instructions from Iran. The latter refused to participate in the conflict, accusing Hamas of hastily and independently resolving the escalating conflict with Israel. Iran is not seeking an open confrontation that might involve the United States.

The situation on Israel's border with Lebanon is unstable, and any skirmish could escalate into a full-scale conflict. Hezbollah is a potential threat because of its arsenal of more than 150 thousand missiles of various ranges and guidance systems. Israeli Defense Minister Yoav Galant warned Hezbollah that if it entered hostilities, Israel would bomb Lebanon into the "stone age."

Hezbollah leader Hassan Nasrallah has threatened Israel with large-scale war, and any serious clash could lead to just that. The near future will show how imminent the danger of war between Israel and Hezbollah is. Sooner or later, Israel must solve this problem. Hezbollah is an aggressive enemy on the country's northern border, much more dangerous than Hamas on Israel's southern border.

A war with Hamas, Hezbollah, or any other jihadist group is essentially a religious war. Islamists are convinced of the superiority of the religion of Islam over all other religions and use the most radical, brutal terrorist methods to achieve their goals. Islamists find support among the poorest and least-educated segments of the population.

Radical Islamists advocate a return to the pure Islam that was practiced in the first centuries of its existence. They believe that Islam has a vital role to play in implementing the laws prescribed by Islam. Islamism is a religious and political movement wing of Islam. It is the desire to drag society back to the moral and religious foundations of the legal system, following the laws of the Koran. Every person would be required to submit to Sharia or die. Hamas (Islamic Resistance Movement) is the Palestinian branch of the Egyptian terrorist cell known as the Muslim Brotherhood. The latter sought to eliminate non-Islamic governments and create a "Great Islamic Caliphate." The Egyptian government has declared the Muslim Brotherhood a terrorist party.

The Israeli government has set as its goal the destruction of the political and military leadership of Hamas. This is the only way to bring peace to the Gaza Strip.

* * *

Hamas, Hezbollah, the Muslim Brotherhood, and other groups represent fanatical Islam. Islamic clerics are engaged in incitement in the Islamic world by claiming that Muhammad ascended to heaven through the Temple Mount in Jerusalem. Muhammad's wife said of his ascent to heaven via the Temple Mount: "It was a dream, not a real event."

Koran (Chapter 7, verse 137) ... it is said that "Allah will bequeath Eretz Israel to the Jewish people, its eastern and western parts," thereby fulfilling the promise given to the Jews.

The roots of hatred of Jews in Christian countries lie in the teachings of the Christian church, which did not want competitors in the struggle for the souls of believers. Jews were called "murderers" of Jesus Christ, spawn of the devil, and guilty of ritual murders of Christian babies. The roots of hatred of Jews in

Islam are associated with the reluctance of Jewish clans to recognize Muhammad as a prophet.

Maimonides: "...As a punishment for our sins, God has thrown us to the mercy of this people, the people of Ishmael (that is, the Muslims), who persistently persecute us, develop ways to harm us and ways to humiliate us... No nation has ever caused more harm to Israel. Nobody wanted to humiliate him like that. No one could humiliate us as they did... We endured their desire for our violent degradation, their lies, their absurdities that went beyond human capabilities... Despite this, we are not spared from the ferocity of their malice. Anytime. On the contrary, the more we suffer and try to give in to them, the more militant and aggressive they become towards us."

Israel's war with Hamas skirts the following boundaries: civilization-barbarism, homophobia-tolerance, cruelty-mercy, evil-good, hatred-compassion, religious intolerance-religious tolerance, multiculturalism-segregation, the desire to kill-compassion...and so on. Hamas soldiers are brutal murderers who hate everything and anything to do with Jews. Rapists of women, children, and men: this is something that the civilized world should reject with disgust. The perverted brain of a savage pushes Islamists to self-destruction in the name of faith in their god, who will meet them in the next world and reward each with seventy-two innocent Gurias. It must be explained that this is simply a beautiful (depending on who it is for) fairy tale but also a senseless and naive one. The blind leading the deaf is a bloody irony of fate. The Jews brought faith in one God to this world. In return, they received thousands of years of suffering, contempt, persecution, gas chambers, and thousands of years of hatred. That is how our world works. Civilization began with the construction of temples to worship the gods. In the name of God, five thousand years later, our species, Homo sapiens, is destroying itself.

* * *

By the seventy-sixth day of Israel's war against Hamas, the civilized world is demanding a ceasefire from Israel. The world is concerned about civilians affected by war. Nobody wants innocent people to die—children, women, older adults, and others who did not take part in the murder of Israelis. Islamic states could solve this problem relatively quickly. They could give refuge to Palestinian citizens, at least while the war is going on, to save their brothers and sisters in faith from the "horrors of the Israeli army." But for some peculiar reason, all Islamist brothers refuse to provide shelter to the suffering Palestinians. The answer lies on the surface: they have already tried to accept the Palestinians.

The PLO (Palestine Liberation Organization), led by Yasser Arafat, tried to seize power in Jordan. The Jordanian Armed Forces drove the PLO forces out of its territory. By 1970, approximately four hundred thousand Palestinians were living in Lebanon. The PLO controlled the southern part of Lebanon, expelling the Lebanese population from there. In 2008, civil war broke out in Lebanon between Christians and Palestinians.

In 1983, the PLO, led by Yasser Arafat, came into conflict with Syrian leader Hafez al-Assad.

After Yasser Arafat's hostile speeches against the Egyptian President, Gamal Abdel Nasser expelled many PLO members from Egypt.

In 1993, the PLO officially announced that it was abandoning its desire to destroy Israel. The PLO has observer status at the UN. There are opinions from Middle East experts who claim that the PLO supports terrorism. The terrorist Islamist groups Hamas and "Islamic Jihad" see the PLO as the enemy, considering the latter traitorous and an appeaser of the main enemy of Islam: the state of Israel.

Every twenty years, a new generation grows up and absorbs with its mother's milk the legacy of hatred of Israel. The dream of the younger generation is becoming a martyr, taking with them as many Israeli lives as possible. Children are taught to hate the Israeli "oppressors." Traditionally, after a terrorist attack on the Palestinian Authority, sweets are distributed. Shahid's parents receive a monthly salary from the PLO administration. Jihad (holy war) is a battle with infidels, an active struggle for Muslim values. For radical Islamists, this is a war of Muslims against non-believers in Islam. That is the reality of the relationship between Israelis and Palestinians.

Palestinians

Palestinians are an ethnic group inhabiting Palestine and its occupied territories, such as the Gaza Strip and the West Bank. Palestinians have a national identity as well as diverse political and religious beliefs. Hamas is one of the Palestinian political and Islamist organizations that is fighting for the liberation of Palestine from the so-called Israeli occupation and the creation of an Islamic state throughout the entire territory, "from the river to the sea (this means from Jordan river to the Mediterranean sea." For them, the Jewish state must be terminated.

On October 7, 2023, having broken through border barriers, Hamas armed forces, numbering more than 2,500 militants, invaded Israeli territory, carrying out a massacre at a music festival that took place near the border with the Gaza Strip and in nearby settlements and military installations. More than 1,200 people died. Hamas bandits captured more than 250 hostages (the data is still being analyzed), women, men, children, and older adults. The Israeli government has declared war on terrorists. Most Arab and Muslim countries blamed Israel, saying Israel's occupation of Palestinian territories caused the conflict.

At the beginning of May 2024, the war between the state of Israel and the Hamas group took on a positional character on the approaches to the city of Rafah. Israel found itself under unprecedented pressure from all sides. Hamas does not want to release the hostages, realizing that this is the only thing keeping Israel from the destruction of the group locked in Rafah. The US, EU, international community, and Arab countries are demanding that Israel end the war, citing concerns about the suffering of Palestinian civilians.

Israel is moving the population of the enclave to prepared tent cities, where the necessary conditions for temporary stay have been created. There are hospitals, food supplies, water, etc.

The situation in Israel and the Gaza Strip is tense. Rafah is a strategic location; a potential attack could further increase tensions. US pressure on Israel is a critical factor in resolving such conflicts.

Student riots in the United States, initiated by Hamas supporters, further complicate this situation. However, it is essential to remember that domestic protests in the United States generally do not have a direct impact on U.S. foreign security policy, including relations with Israel.

The international community usually expresses grave concern about using force in such conflicts and calls for dialogue and peaceful resolution.

The problem of Israeli hostages in the hands of groups such as Hamas poses a severe threat to Israel's security. Freeing hostages is a complex process that requires diplomatic efforts, including negotiations, prisoner exchanges, or even special operations.

Israel generally seeks the release of its citizens in captivity and is willing to take various measures to secure their freedom. That could mean negotiations with intermediaries, prisoner exchanges, or special operations to free hostages.

However, resolving this problem can be complicated by political and security considerations and requires careful balancing between humanitarian considerations and danger to the hostage.

The confrontation between Israel and Hamas in the struggle for control of Rafah could have several possible outcomes:

Military offensive and Israeli capture of Rafah: This scenario could result in significant casualties on both sides, as well as further escalation of the conflict between Israel and the Palestinians. It could also provoke a harsh reaction from the international community and heightened criticism of Israel.

Diplomatic settlement: The parties may be able to reach a diplomatic agreement that will avoid military confrontation and resolve the Rafah dispute peacefully. That may include seeking a final solution to the conflict from other states or international organizations.

Temporary truce or ceasefire: The parties may agree to a temporary truce or ceasefire to prevent the conflict around Rafah from escalating. That could temporarily pause diplomatic efforts and negotiations to release the hostages.

The conflict around Rafah may end without significant changes, leaving the territory under one of the parties' control or in a disputed status. That may temporarily ease tensions but will not solve the underlying problems of the conflict.

The resolution of the conflict in Rafah depends on several factors, the main one being the release of Israeli hostages. Israel plays a crucial role in resolving the conflict, as it controls the border with the Gaza Strip and has a military presence in the Rafah area. Israel's decisions and actions can significantly influence the development of the situation.

Hamas and other Palestinian groups still control parts of the Gaza Strip and have significant influence over the residents of the area. Hamas' decisions and actions could also determine the course of the conflict in Rafah.

Many countries and international organizations are interested in resolving the conflict between Israel and Hamas. They can provide diplomatic support, medicine, and resources to help resolve the situation in Rafah.

Regional countries such as Egypt, Qatar, Turkey, and Saudi Arabia can also influence the resolution of the Rafah conflict through diplomacy, mediation, and financial support.

Ultimately, resolving the Rafah conflict requires a concerted effort by all parties involved, including Israel, Hamas, the international community, and regional players. Muslim countries can play a crucial role in resolving the conflict between Israel and Hamas, as they are essential players in the region and have influence on various sides of the conflict.

Qatar often acts as a mediator and provides financial support to Hamas. He may participate in diplomatic efforts to achieve a truce or peaceful solution to the conflict. Qatar sponsors Hamas, which gives it some influence over the group and can be used as a means of promoting a peace settlement.

Egypt also plays a key role because it has a long history of mediating conflicts between Israel and Palestinian factions, including Hamas. Egypt can help organize negotiations and facilitate the conclusion of a truce. Egypt also controls the border with the Gaza Strip and can put pressure on Hamas if necessary.

Turkey generally supports the Palestinians, including Hamas, and can provide political and diplomatic support to the Palestinian side and express their opinion on resolving the conflict. Turkey often criticizes Israel for its actions. It can use its political and diplomatic influence on the Palestinian side to help resolve the conflict.

Although a US ally that has no diplomatic relations with Israel, Saudi Arabia could also play a role in resolving the conflict by acting as a mediator or providing diplomatic support to peace efforts.

Although Saudi Arabia does not have diplomatic relations with Israel, it partially coordinates security issues with the Saudis and also advocates for the rights of Palestinians. Its influence can be used to support the peace process and conflict resolution.

"Peace in the Middle East will come when Arabs love their children more than they hate Jews." - Golda Meir.

* * *

On Friday, October 27, at an extraordinary meeting, the UN General Assembly adopted a resolution on the situation in the Gaza Strip. The document calls for "an immediate, permanent, and sustainable ceasefire leading to a cessation of hostilities."

The UN replaced the League of Nations, which was organized in 1920 at the Paris Peace Conference. The League of Nations was created during the First World War "to promote cooperation among nations and ensure peace and security." It ceased to exist in 1946 due to its failure to prevent the Second World War, which caused enormous loss of life (50-80 million people).

Over the seventy-five years of its existence, the UN has become a platform for condemning Israel. The organization, which includes 193 UN member states, did not recognize the Hamas terrorist attack in the text of the resolution on the situation in the Gaza Strip. UN Secretary-General Antonio Guterres criticized the bombing of the Gaza Strip and called for a humanitarian ceasefire, the release of hostages, and assistance to the population.

Between 2015 and 2022, the UN General Assembly adopted 140 resolutions criticizing Israel.

Peace and tranquility will come to this world if Russia stops killing people in Ukraine.

Peace and tranquility will come to this world if Iran stops using its proxies (trusted, authorized) to attack other countries.

Peace and tranquility will come to this world if North Korea stops threatening its neighbors with nuclear weapons.

Peace and tranquility will come to this world if:

South Sudan...

Democratic Republic of Congo...

Iraq…

Yemen…

Somalia…

Venezuela…

Nigeria…

South Africa …

And other countries will become normal civilized countries where the rights of others are respected, and governments care about the population's well-being.

Will the descendants of ferocious primitive apes be able to become just people?

Faith-Religion-Ideology

Beginning

Modern Islamic fundamentalism, directed against the Western world and its way of life, is another example of the manifestation of the ideological essence of religion.

Anthropogenesis is part of biological evolution that led to the emergence of Homo sapiens, a species that separated from other hominids. Any biological species goes through the formation of particular mutations in natural selection associated with the struggle for existence. The origin of man from the monkey has been proven by science. Still, no scientific evidence exists for religion, believing communities convinced of the first man's divine creation in God's image and likeness.

In *The Origin of Species*, Charles Darwin hypothesized man's origin from apes. The vast majority of modern scientists believe that our species, Homo sapiens, developed, like other species of monkeys, as a result of natural selection. That is a struggle for survival when those most adapted to certain geographical and natural conditions survive. A species exists as long as its offspring reproduce. The competition mechanism for a sexual partner is embedded in the limbic system of our species, which stimulates selective mating and causes the natural selection of the fittest offspring. Caring for offspring exists in almost all extant species of living organisms.

Scientists tell us about the first typical representative of the ancestors of ancient apes, Archaebas, who lived in Africa fifty-five million years ago. The biological species closest to modern humans is the chimpanzee. The evolution of humans and chimpanzees split about seven million years ago. Our ancestors lived in the crowns of tall trees, eating the bark, leaves, and fruits of the trees on which they lived. Breeding in favorable conditions of a warm climate, they were cheerful, carefree creatures with a brain size of four hundred to five hundred grams. Time passed, and climate-related changes in nature transformed the habitat. The trees became sparse and low, which forced the monkeys to look for another way to survive. They descended to the ground for food and had to stand on their hind legs, walking from rare trees to other trees in search of food. The freed front paws were adapted for searching and holding plants, berries, fruits, and anything edible. The food was supplemented with meat abandoned by predators. Eating raw meat promotes brain growth. The monkeys became predators, hunting other inhabitants to kill and eat. Of the numerous species of apes, the species that we today call "Homo sapiens" has been preserved.

About two million years ago, the species Homo erectus began migrating from the African continent. The environment had changed. The usual places with familiar, abundant food had disappeared. In search of food, they had to travel long distances.

The fauna of Africa left the continent in search of food and better living conditions. Among them were representatives of several species of primitive people at different stages of development. Science has counted more than twenty similar species. Today we know that one species survived: Homo sapiens. In Israel, the remains of representatives of Homo sapiens, who migrated from Africa 185 thousand years ago, were found. There is also evidence of earlier migrations.

Our species ate plant foods and hunted representatives of the animal world. Such a transition from eating plant foods to meat allowed Homo sapiens to obtain a large brain with a volume of 1650 cm³. For the reasons that are still unclear to us, the volume of the brain of our species has decreased over time by 50 cm³ to 250 cm³. We will not posit the reasons here but will try to figure out how they ate. Scientists say that our distant ancestors were omnivorous hunter-gatherers. To support this way of life, tribal communities traveled long distances searching for edible food: roots, fruits, leaves, and grains.

Hunting and the appearance of stone tools made it possible to obtain meat from animals and birds. Life on the shores of seas and rivers made it possible to diversify the diet with fish and seafood.

When did our distant ancestors start speaking? Living in communities, they involuntarily communicated using gestures and sounds. Each community developed certain sounds and gestures that were understandable to clan members. The large brain remembered repeated sounds, generating specific images associated with certain sounds. The emerging thought, conveyed by gesture or sound, created an image of what a community member was trying to say. This information concerns the danger or possibility of moving toward an area with edible plants. This incredible ability to transmit by sound what became visible turned primitive man into a thinking being. That was a giant step that made man the master of the earth. So far, this "master" has presented an image this not very impressionable. Overgrown with thick hair, with a stick or stone in his hands, he rummaged in the ground in search of edible root vegetables. But he already knew how to hunt large animals, coordinating his actions with other clan members and creating a specific strategy for attacking the chosen target. The animal, after being killed, became the subject of triumph and pride that the hunters felt when they brought the prey to the camp. The rest of the clan praised the brave hunters who shared their catch with the clan members. Songs and dances were born that reflected all the vicissitudes of hunting and killing the intended victim.

If a successful hunt brought food for a certain period, then an unsuccessful one could end in the death of one or more clan members. Then there were sad, bitter lamentations and tears of farewell. The dead were buried in caves or other places following the rites of the clan. The veneration of the dead created the idea of a mysterious other world where the deceased member of the clan lived after earthly life.

Early forms of religious beliefs in mysterious deities inhabiting the afterlife arose. Fear of otherworldly forces and the possible influence of powerful deities on every person's daily life gave rise to faith and worship of these unknown forces.

Fear of the unknown and the need to explain incomprehensible events gave rise to myths and belief in gods, which explained the events occurring in the world in which our ancestors lived.

* * *

Religion-ideology: in previous volumes of the series, we have already touched on this topic. What does this pairing have in common?

Essentially, these concepts are equivalent. Our species, Homo sapiens, created religion. That was an inevitable stage in the history of the development of the human brain. The evolution of our species took place over millions of years. The awakening consciousness demanded an explanation of what was happening around them, and the first communities (flocks) of primitive people tried to stay together in small groups. These communities, led by the most muscular male of the pack (community), developed specific principles and rules that subordinated the community and explained the phenomena around it. Belief in gods was widespread among primitive peoples. An object or image of worship endowed with mystical power is a deity made sacred, possessing all-pervading magical power. A natural step in worshiping powerful forces that could affect the life of any being was the worship of deceased members of the tribal family.

The totems of the community were deified and endowed with supernatural properties. These totems or deities required awe, obedience, the performance of certain rituals, and the worship of mythological forces that could influence life and death. Totemism, the first form of religion of a primitive community, is the awe of a chosen totem as a deity capable of protecting or punishing anyone who violates established rules. This concept was based on mythological explanations of natural phenomena occurring and the birth and death of community members, who could influence the community's well-being through mythical forces.

The feeling of helplessness in the face of natural phenomena required an explanation of these phenomena and the opportunity, if not to control, then at least to ask for help and forgiveness for an unwittingly committed offense in front of the totem or an accidental violation of the adoration of the totem and taboo (religious prohibition). The deification of the forces of nature and the worship of totems led to the creation of rules of obedience and worship of deities that allegedly controlled the forces of nature through their representatives (totems). Violating a taboo (prohibition) could harm the entire community, so the punishment was more severe. Naturally, individuals who pretended to be messengers of almighty forces and deities appeared.

Along with totemism, the oldest type of religious faith was shamanism. Performing various ritual dances, accompanied by the beating of tambourines or other resonating objects, the shamans fell into feigned or natural ecstasy. Waking up from ecstasy, they told the gullible savages about visiting distant worlds and meeting the gods.

Shamans also engaged in healing ailments, explaining the reasons for violations of the rules of veneration of mysterious forces, which can be corrected by paying a certain fee for ritual services.

In the clan hierarchy, the shaman could be a leader or a subordinate of the leading leader. It could have been the other way around when the leader bowed his head to the shaman. A similar hierarchy was preserved in further forms of religious communities.

Fear and helplessness before the formidable phenomena of nature demanded the worship and humanization of these forces, which became gods. Thunderstorms, lightning, downpours, high mountains, huge stones or trees, predators prowling in search of food, the leader of a pack (community): all of these could become objects of worship or deities.

Worship and hope for leniency gave community members hope for protection and patronage.

In their development, human communities acquired specific knowledge about natural phenomena, which could replace the worship of the forces of nature with new religious ideas about the structure of the surrounding world, faith in the almighty gods of our world, perfect and fair. The large brain of man gave birth to (the invented) belief in supernatural gods who need to be revered and pleased. Without exception, all religious beliefs are illusions of our consciousness in the face of fear of punishment in the present or afterlife. In any religion, the main thing is faith, service to the chosen deity, and fear of the afterlife. The human brain has created an imaginary world that has become the reality of the consciousness of the species Homo sapiens. Believers always react militantly to criticism and are intolerant of doubt.

All favorable events that have occurred or have successfully resolved problems are attributed to correctly performed rituals. Religion explains all the cataclysms and disasters that occur through unbelief, wrong, sinful actions and thoughts. Religion requires the believer to perform certain rituals, a violation of which is considered a sin. Ministers of religious worship occupy a special place. They are considered devoted and inspired servants of the gods and teachers who have achieved holiness and the highest spiritual state.

Ideology is associated with processes occurring in real life, and religion is based on the afterlife and the psychological preparation of a person for the transition to another state. Ideologies, like religions, are tools with which one can control huge masses of obedient people who sincerely believe in religious (ideological) dogmas and promises. Fear of punishment in the afterlife—or, conversely, the promise of a paradisical afterlife—is an effective tool for a dependent psyche, ready to atone for sin at any cost or earn forgiveness.

* * *

One of the first religious beliefs came in the form of polytheism: the belief in numerous gods. Primitive man believed in various spirits extant in living nature and material objects. Polytheism assumed a hierarchy of different deities exerting a specific influence on some regions of nature and society. At the head of the pantheon is a supreme god, often the sun god. The mythology of polytheism offers the origin story of the universe and the places of man in it. Cult servants performed various rituals of worshiping the gods to obtain a favorable result for the worshipers.

Numerous polytheistic religious systems still exist today: Buddhism, Hinduism, Taoism, Shintoism, traditional African religions, and many others.

Monotheistic religion, the belief in one God, has supplanted polytheism to become the most powerful form of religion in the world. Scientists consider Zoroastrianism one of the first monotheistic beliefs, the ancient religion of the Iranian people. Ahura Mazda was the supreme god in Zoroastrianism, and he communicated with the prophet Zarathustra.

The Jewish people believe that they founded a monotheistic religion. The Tanakh, the Pentateuch of Moses, and the Holy Scriptures entered the Christian Bible as the Old Testament. The Christian religion has become the most widespread religion in the world.

Almost seven hundred years later, another Abrahamic monotheistic religion emerged: Islam.

The largest religious community today is Christianity, accounting for 33 percent of the world's religious population. The second most popular world religion is Islam, with about 23 percent of the population.

* * *

Does religion have a positive impact on the development of our species? Without a doubt, yes. In the early stages of our species, shared rituals and the worship of certain creeds strengthened the community, allowing for the observance of accepted rituals and social behavior. The community of faith created moral and ethical standards that supported generally accepted rules that created the stability of the community. The community's religious life supported psychological well-being by addressing issues of meaning in life, justice, life, and death. Being in such a community provides confidence in safety.

In the later stages of developing our species, religion-created traditions made particular education possible and allowed the preservation of cultural values. Our species owes its existence to religion, the appearance of the first temples for worship and religious ceremonies. Temples became the centers of emerging settlements. They were built for religious rites, ceremonies, prayers, and deity worship. Temples became the centers of social life of the community, where festive events were held, sacrifices were made, and served as a place of communication with deities for forgiveness and help.

Temples became more and more majestic and required architectural and artistic skill. Many temples became grandiose and iconic structures. The temples owned lands, sacred wells, and canals used to irrigate fertile soil. Temple servants appointed military leaders in case of war and kept records of leased land plots. The temples housed valuable art, religious artifacts, and sacred texts.

Leaders sought approval and strengthening of their position from religious authorities. It was a mutually beneficial collaboration. Religious leaders helped legitimize power, receiving in return funding for temple construction, generous donations, and religious devotion.

Religiosity and belief in the divine origin of man have been preserved for thousands of years. The longevity of religious rituals, texts, and traditions is associated with the human need for a fundamental belief in justice and retribution, if not in this world, then at least in the other world. Religion gave believers answers to fundamental questions about the origin, meaning of life, moral rules, and life after death. Religion shapes social order, ethical norms, and moral principles.

Religion helps cope with shocks and fears and provides comfort. Religious practices are a source of hope and support. A person is associated with religion from the moment of birth until the moment of death. In moments of weakness and in a search for answers to the essential questions of life, a religious person turns to his god with a prayer for help. Religion teaches that God hears all prayers. This faith helps people to survive difficult moments since the hope is that a person's prayers will be heard: "... and he will be rewarded according to his faith...". Modern people today turn to psychologists for help with their problems. Turning to his god, a religious person experiences spiritual strength, support, and inner peace through communication with God. Although there is no specific answer, such communication helps to strengthen faith in divine plans and intentions. The positive influence of religion on human consciousness is carried out in providing moral guidelines and meaning in life.

Without a doubt, religious influence also has opposing sides, ranging from religious conflicts to discrimination and restrictions on freedom of thought. The influence of religion on Homo sapiens depends on specific religious beliefs, interpretations, and interactions with social, cultural, and personal circumstances. Religious fanaticism leads to extremism. While in this state, people, due to their beliefs, can commit violent terrorist acts and persecute representatives of other religions.

Such intolerant religious teachings, while suppressing critical thinking, require the acceptance of established dogmas without any critical analysis or questioning. The formation of such communities leads to the prohibition of doubts about the correctness of declared beliefs.

Some religious teachings encourage discrimination based on gender, sexual orientation, race, or other characteristics. Religious teachings may conflict with scientific knowledge, which leads to distortion of the educational process, especially in the field of natural sciences.

Strict religious teachings can make believers feel guilty, fearful, or sinful. The influence of such religious teachings can lead to irreversible mental consequences for believers, especially if this requires unconditional adherence to dogmas and declared truths. In the later stages of the development of our species, religion created traditions and specific education and helped preserve cultural values.

It is essential to highlight that religion can also positively impact many people's lives by providing them with moral guidance, community, and meaning in life. The influence of religion on a person's consciousness varies greatly and depends on many factors, including personal choice and context.

Religious teachings and ideologies can promote military conflicts. Religious beliefs have always played a key role in sparking conflict in Europe, the Middle East, South Asia, and other regions. Religious leaders and organizations influence the formation of peace initiatives or the incitement of conflicts. Religious beliefs have historically played a significant role in forming interstate and intrastate relations, often becoming a catalyst for military conflicts. Differences in religious views can lead to deep divisions between peoples, cultures, and countries, causing clashes that sometimes escalate into large-scale wars. At the same time, religion can be a powerful tool for peacebuilding and reconciliation.

The history of humankind contains examples of when religious motives became the cause or significant intensification of hostilities. The Crusades (1096–1291) are one of the most famous examples where religious beliefs led to a series of military campaigns by Christian Europe against Muslims in the Middle East. In modern times, religious wars in Europe, including the Thirty Years' War (1618–1648), were also caused by religious differences. These conflicts show how religious beliefs can mobilize the masses, form alliances, and lead to deadly clashes.

Today's wars related to religious or ideological motives threaten world order and the existence of states with millions of people. Increasingly sophisticated means of exterminating people for religious or ideological reasons threaten the mutual destruction of the species Homo sapiens itself.

Religious teachings and ideologies can influence adherents' perceptions of war and peace. For example, the concept of "holy war" is present in some religious traditions and can be interpreted as a call for armed struggle against "unholy opponents of the true deity." However, many religions also preach peace and tolerance, emphasizing the need for peaceful coexistence and mutual understanding. Different interpretations of religious texts and teachings can lead to opposing views on the justification of military action.

In the modern world, religious beliefs continue to instigate and influence military conflicts. For example, the confrontation between Israel and Palestine, conflicts in Iraq and Syria, between Iran and Israel, and tension between India and Pakistan have a religious component. Such clashes demonstrate how religious dogma and beliefs exacerbate geopolitical and ethnic divisions.

Religious leaders and organizations play a dual role in the context of military conflicts. On the one hand, they can call for peace and tolerance, using their influence to reduce tensions and mediate peace negotiations. On the other hand, some religious leaders may incite violence by using religious rhetoric to justify military action and mobilize their followers.

Interreligious dialogue and cooperation can be a powerful tool for preventing conflict and promoting peace. Examples of successful initiatives, such as peace talks between religious groups in Ireland and interfaith meetings to reduce tensions in the Central African Republic, show that joint efforts can lead to sustainable peace and understanding.

Religious conflicts in India between Hindus and Muslims led to the partition of India and the creation of Pakistan in 1947. These long-standing religious tensions could lead to large-scale geopolitical changes and long-term conflicts.

Contemporary conflict in Syria, where religious differences between Sunnis, Shiites, and other groups have a complicated military confrontation and external powers have exploited religious differences to advance their interests. Religious extremism from groups such as the Islamic State has helped fuel conflicts. The role of religious organizations such as the Vatican and the Organization of Islamic Cooperation can help international peacebuilding and conflict resolution efforts. There are examples where these organizations initiated and supported peace negotiations and dialogue between conflicting parties.

Modern media and social networks influence the perception and dissemination of religious beliefs related to the conflict, spreading extremist ideology. It is difficult to overstate the importance of a profound understanding of religious beliefs and interreligious dialogue in preventing conflict and building sustainable peace. The challenge today is to reduce religious tensions and promote peaceful coexistence. Religious beliefs profoundly influence military conflicts, acting as catalysts for conflict.

Russia

Modern Russia is the historical heir to previous forms of statehood in the ninth century. The Old Russian state arose on the lands of the East Slavic tribes, on the trade route "from the Varangians to the Greeks." Kyivan Rus was formed in the ninth century, uniting the East Slavic and Finno-Ugric tribes under the rule of the Rurik princes. The Principality of Kyiv remained in the possession of the Russian princes. The main population were peasants. This population had no rights and often became enslaved people for debt. The common language, Old Russian, goes back to the Proto-Slavic language.

Prince Oleg captured Kyiv in 882, killing its rulers. The phrase is attributed to him: "Behold, the mother of the Russian city." Kyiv received the status of an "all-Russian" capital. The second city was considered Novgorod in the north of the country. By the Mongol invasion in the thirteenth century, Kyivan Rus consisted of more than three hundred cities.

The army of Ancient Rus was mercenary, most of which were Varangians. The princes' squads were scattered over a vast territory, practically unconnected with each other. The central part of the army was the militia. Poorly armed and poorly trained.

The monarchy in Russia began to take shape during the period of Kyivan Rus. Finally, it took shape under Ivan III (1462-1505), who significantly expanded the state's territory and laid the foundations of a centralized state. His grandson Ivan IV (Ivan the Terrible) became the first Russian Tsar in 1547, symbolizing the further strengthening of monarchical power. Under him, the Oprichnina was introduced. The guardsmen are the sovereign's people who made up the personal guard of Tsar Ivan Vasilyevich. The educated Oprichnina army performed security, surveillance, investigative, and punitive functions. The guardsmen were distinguished by the fact that while riding, they had dog heads tied to the horse's neck and a broom on their whip. These images symbolize dog bites and a broom that cleanses everything unnecessary from the country. The Oprichina took a personal oath of allegiance to the tsar. This particular army was created to fight the gentry because of Ivan the Terrible's suspicions of betraying the gentry in favor of the Polish king. Torture and executions accompanied Grozny's campaign against Novgorod and Pskov, and the cruelty with which the guardsmen dealt with the enemies of the sovereign led to thousands of deaths, famine, disease, and plague. Repression continued against people close to the tsar and leaders of the Oprichina. In Moscow, convicts were executed; oprichniki executioners stabbed, chopped, hanged, and poured boiling water over the condemned. The tsar took a personal part in the executions, and crowds of Oprichnina greeted the executions with shouts. Wives, children, and family members were persecuted. Ivan the Terrible came up with unique methods of torment: hot frying pans, ovens, tongs, rubbing the body with thin ropes, etc.

The Oprichnina existed until the death of Ivan the Terrible in 1584.

Throughout its history, the Russian state has pursued an active expansionist policy. Significant conquests began during Ivan III, who expanded the state's borders to include most of the Novgorod land. Ivan IV continued this tradition, waging long and bloody wars for control of the Kazan and Astrakhan khanates, which led to the expansion of Russian lands to the east. Later, during the Romanov era, Russia significantly expanded its borders by conquering Siberia and wars in Europe and the Caucasus.

The situation of peasants in Russia worsened significantly in the sixteenth century when serfdom was introduced. That meant the peasants were tied to the land, and the landowner had no right to leave the land without the owner's permission and practically became enslaved people. Serfdom was finally enshrined in the "Cathedral Code" of 1649. From this point until the abolition of serfdom in 1861, the situation of the peasants remained complicated, with limited rights and significant responsibilities.

After the abolition of serfdom in 1861, significant socio-economic changes occurred, but monarchical power remained until the early twentieth century. There were several dynasties on the Russian throne, but the reign of the Romanovs, which began in 1613 and lasted until 1917, was especially significant. During this period, the Russian Empire reached the peak of its territorial expansion and international influence, but internal problems and social discontent accumulated. An active foreign policy and numerous wars marked the eighteenth and nineteenth centuries. Peter I (Peter the Great) reformed the army and navy, which made it possible to successfully conduct the Northern War

(1700-1721) and gain access to the Baltic Sea. Catherine II (Catherine the Great) continued her expansionist policies, significantly expanding Russia's borders in the south and west, including the annexation of Crimea, parts of Poland, and new territories in the Caucasus. In the nineteenth century, Russia continued its territorial expansion in Central Asia, the Caucasus, and the Far East. The abolition of serfdom in 1861 formally freed the peasants from serfdom, but they faced new problems. Most of the land remained in the hands of the landowners, and the peasants were forced to buy back the land at inflated prices, which led to deepening their debt and dependence. Economic difficulties, coupled with limited political freedoms, contributed to growing social discontent, which ultimately led to the revolutionary events of the early twentieth century.

* * *

The accumulated socioeconomic contradictions and failures in foreign policy, including defeat in the Russo-Japanese War (1904-1905) and the consequences of participation in the First World War, undermined the monarchy's authority. The February Revolution of 1917 overthrew Emperor Nicholas II, ending more than three hundred years of rule by the House of Romanov in Russia.

The revolution created a provisional government that attempted to govern the country amid political instability and ongoing war. However, the inability of the Provisional Government to solve pressing socioeconomic problems and lead the country out of the First World War led to the growing popularity of the Bolshevik Party, which promised peace, land, and bread.

Karl Marx
From Marxism to communism

Karl Marx (1818-1883) was a German philosopher born into a Jewish family, an economist, a political theorist, and one of the founders of Marxism. His theories of capitalism and class struggle had a significant influence on the development of socialist and communist ideas throughout the world. Marxism offers a critical analysis of capitalism as an economic system in which the means of production are privately owned, and the working class's labor is exploited in the interests of capital accumulation.

Marx's theory of communism seeks to create a society in which there are no classes, no state, and ownership of the means of production is public. In such a society, each person contributes according to their abilities and receives according to their needs. The main provisions of his theory are set out in the works *Manifesto of the Communist Party* (together with Friedrich Engels) and *Capital*.

In the *Communist Manifesto*, published in 1848, Marx and Engels outlined the basic principles of Marxism, including the ideas of class struggle, historical materialism, and the need for a proletarian revolution to create a communist society. Capitalism analyzes the capitalist system, emphasizing the exploitation of the working class and predicting its inevitable collapse due to internal contradictions.

Marx argued that capitalism creates deep social inequality and that only a radical transformation of the economic structure of society through revolution can lead to a socialist and, ultimately, communist system. That entails the abolition of private ownership of the means of production and the establishment of the dictatorship of the proletariat as a transitional stage to the construction of a communist society.

Marxism had a significant influence on the development of political thought and practice in the twentieth century, inspiring many socialist revolutions and movements around the world, including revolutions in Russia, North Korea, China, Cuba, Venezuela, and other countries. However, implementing Marx's ideas in these countries often deviated from his original theories, which led to the creation of various forms of socialism.

Critics of Marxism point out several supposed errors and shortcomings in Karl Marx's theory. However, it is essential to note that assessing these "mistakes" can vary significantly depending on ideological, economic, and philosophical views. Below are some aspects that are often highlighted as significant shortcomings or errors of Marxist theory:

Marx focused on class struggle and economic structures, while critics argue that individual choice and innovation play a crucial role in economic development and social progress.

Marx predicted that capitalism would inevitably be destroyed due to internal contradictions and intensifying class struggle. However, capitalism continues to exist and adapt, demonstrating the ability to reform and innovate.

Marxist theory is often criticized for overemphasizing economic factors as the main driving forces of history and society while minimizing the role of culture, ideology, and politics.

The history of the twentieth century has shown that attempts to implement Marxist ideas often led to dictatorship, human rights violations, and economic difficulties, which cast doubt on the possibility of creating an ideal communist society without classes and a state.

Marx proposed the concept of the "dictatorship of the proletariat" as a transitional stage to communism. In practice, this often led to authoritarian regimes approved by the authorities in the name of the proletariat but suppressed political diversity and civil liberties.

That and other criticisms reflect the complexity and contradictions of Marxist theory. However, it is worth noting that Marxism is not a monolithic doctrine, and its interpretations and adaptations vary considerably. Many followers of Marx recognize the potential shortcomings of his theory and propose various ways to overcome them or modify the main provisions.

Continuing the analysis of the main criticisms of Marxism, we can consider the following aspects and the development of critical thought with Marx's theory:

Marx predicted increased exploitation and worsening living conditions of the working class under capitalism, which would lead to unification and revolution. However, in many developed countries, the standard of living of the working class has improved significantly, and the welfare state has helped alleviate some of the most pressing problems predicted by Marx.

Implementing Marxist ideas in the Soviet Union and other countries in the form of central planning and state control of the economy led to inefficiency, commodity shortages, and the suppression of economic initiative.

The original works of Marx and Engels paid little attention to the problems of the environment and sustainable development, which is one of the critical challenges of the modern world.

Marx presented a vision of a future communist society in which all social injustice and economic problems would be eliminated. Critics argue that such a vision is too utopian and does not consider the complexity of human nature and social relations.

Marx outlined the general contours of the transformation of society toward communism but gave few details about exactly how this transition should be carried out, which leaves many questions about the practical implementation of his ideas.

It is essential to understand that Marxism is not a static doctrine. Over time, many thinkers have developed and modified Marxist theory to respond to criticism and adapt it to changing conditions. For example, neo-Marxism examines society's cultural and ideological aspects, and eco-Marxism incorporates environmental considerations into the analysis of economic systems. These and other directions show the flexibility and adaptability of Marxist thought to the new challenges of our time.

Continuing reflection on the criticism and adaptation of Marxism in the modern world leads us to the following aspects:

Modern sociological research shows that the class structure of society is much more complex than Marxist theory suggests.

The existence of a middle class, professionals, and technicians who do not fit into the categories of "bourgeoisie" or "proletariat" raises questions about the reality of class struggle in its classical Marxist sense.

Marxism has traditionally analyzed capitalism within the framework of the nation-state, but the globalization of the economy characterizes the modern world, the international movement of capital, and labor migration. These processes create new conditions for class struggle and exploitation that require a renewed theoretical approach.

The development of technology and the transition to an information economy are changing the nature of work, creating new forms of production and distribution that Marx could not have foreseen. That raises questions about the applicability of Marxist ideas to the conditions of post-industrial society.

Contemporary social movements often focus on issues of identity, gender, race, and ethnicity, which were not the focus of Marxist theory. That highlights the need to integrate these aspects into socioeconomic analysis.

In many cases, the practical implementation of Marxist ideas in the twentieth century led to establishment of authoritarian regimes, which attracted criticism from liberals and anarchists. Here, the question arises about the correspondence between Marxist theory and its practical results.

Although some of Marx's works contain the seeds of environmental thought, modern Marxism needs to integrate environmental concerns into its analysis to respond to the climate crisis challenges and unsustainable industrial practices.

Developing the discussion about Marxism and its criticism is worth highlighting how modern interpretations and adaptations of Marxist theory are trying to overcome these shortcomings and criticisms and respond to new global challenges.

Modern interpretations and adaptations of Marxism:

Cultural Marxism focuses on analyzing culture and ideology rather than just economic structures, emphasizing the role of hegemony and cultural institutions in maintaining power and inequality.

Eco-Marxism integrates environmental issues into Marxist analysis, criticizing capitalism for its role in the environmental crisis and exploring paths to sustainable socioeconomic development. Post-Marxism moves away from some traditional aspects of Marxism, such as economic determinism, and explores new social movements and identities not limited to class struggle. Analytical Marxism applies the methods of analytical philosophy to rethink Marxist concepts and theories, seeking to make them more accurate and valid.

Modern Marxists recognize the need for a more flexible approach to implementing socialist and communist ideas, including democratic participation and diversity of forms of ownership and governance.

Human nature and socialism: Contrary to arguments that communism is antithetical to human nature, modern theorists point to the historical variability of human social and economic relations and the potential for creating conditions that support more just and equal relationships.

Economic determinism and cultural factors: Recognizing the limitations of strict economic determinism, twenty-first-century Marxism includes a broader analysis of the social, cultural, and ideological factors influencing social processes.

Globalization and international capitalism: Contemporary Marxists actively analyze globalization and its impact on the world economy, class structure, and international relations, exploring new forms of international solidarity and struggle against globalization.

Analyzing criticism in the development of Marxism, we can highlight additional aspects that have become the subject of discussion and reform in the context of modern challenges and criticism. Deep globalization of economics, culture, and politics characterizes the modern world. That creates new conditions for class struggle and international workers' solidarity, which Marx saw in the more limited context of the nineteenth century. Contemporary Marxists examine how globalization affects exploitation, inequality, and the possibilities for international labor solidarity.

Traditional Marxism focused on class struggle and economic relations, leaving issues of gender and sexuality on the periphery. Contemporary Marxist theorists contribute to the development of feminist Marxism, which analyzes the intersection of class and gender inequalities, emphasizing the importance of the struggle for gender equality as part of broader social transformation.

For global environmental issues such as climate change and loss of biodiversity, eco-Marxism offers a rethinking of Marxist theory from an environmental perspective. Eco-Marxists criticize the capitalist system for its mismanagement of natural resources and exploitation of the environment, arguing that only a radical change in the relations of production can lead to an environmentally sustainable society.

For technological change and the future of work, with the Fourth Industrial Revolution and the increasing automation of production, Marxists face questions about the future of work, income distribution, and the role of technology in the economy. In analyzing these changes, modern Marxists examine how new technologies can contribute to the liberation of labor or, conversely, to increased exploitation and inequality.

These areas of research and criticism show that Marxism continues to evolve and adapt to new conditions and challenges. Modern Marxists seek not only to criticize existing social, economic, and political structures but also seek ways to build a more just and sustainable society based on the principles of solidarity, equality, and sustainable development.

Vladimir Lenin

Vladimir Lenin (1870-1924) was a revolutionary figure, political theorist, and founder of the Russian Soviet Federative Socialist Republic (RSFSR), later to become the Soviet Union. Lenin played a vital role in the October Revolution of 1917, which led to the overthrow of the Provisional Government and the establishment of Soviet power. His actions and ideas greatly impacted the development of Marxist theory and the practice of socialism in the twentieth century.

Lenin adapted Marxist theory to the specific sociopolitical conditions of Russia, a country with relatively undeveloped capitalism and a weak proletariat. He developed the concept of a "new type of party": an armed vanguard of the working class, which was supposed to lead the revolution and establish the "dictatorship of the proletariat" in the interests of building socialism and the subsequent transition to communism. This idea was outlined in his work "What Is to Be Done?"

Lenin believed that for the successful implementation of the socialist revolution and the construction of a socialist society, it was necessary to overcome bourgeois statehood and replace it with Soviet power based on unions of workers, peasants, and soldiers. Under his leadership, the Bolsheviks carried out many radical economic and social reforms, including nationalizing land and industry.

The October Revolution, which occurred on October 25 (November 7, new style) 1917, brought the Bolsheviks to power under the leadership of Vladimir Lenin. This event marked the beginning of a civil war that lasted until 1922 and led to the establishment of Soviet power in most of the territory of the former Russian Empire.

The creation of the Soviet Union in 1922 was the realization of the idea of the first state built on Marxist-Leninist principles. Lenin faced many challenges during his reign, including the Civil War, foreign intervention, economic difficulties, and internal political strife. In response to the economic problems caused by the policy of "war communism," Lenin introduced a new economic policy (NEP), which partially restored market relations and private property in agriculture.

Vladimir Lenin left a complex legacy. On the one hand, he was revered as the founder of the first socialist state and the inspirer of communist and anti-colonial movements worldwide. On the other hand, his methods of political struggle, including the use of violence and repression against opponents, still elicit sharp criticism and controversy.

Lenin's interpretation of Marxism and its practical implementation in the form of the Soviet state profoundly influenced world history, especially in the development of communist and socialist movements in the twentieth century. Building on the ideas of Marx and Engels, Lenin introduced critical theoretical and practical ideas that influenced the course of socialist experiments worldwide.

After Lenin died in 1924, his ideas were supplemented and developed within the framework of Leninism, which became the official ideology of the Soviet Union. Leninism emphasized the importance of the revolutionary party as the vanguard of the working class, the need for socialist revolution in countries with backward capitalism, and the strategy for world revolution.

In practical terms, the Leninist model presupposed centralized economic planning, strict control over society's political and social life, and implementing policies aimed at destroying the old bourgeois structures and creating the foundations of a socialist society. However, this model has also faced several criticisms and problems:

The reign of Lenin and subsequent Soviet leaders was often characterized by tight political control, suppression of opposition, and widespread repression.

Central planning and management of the economy led to inefficiency, shortages of goods, and slower innovation.

The idea of the dictatorship of the proletariat led to the emergence of a powerful bureaucratic system, which, according to many critics, moved away from the ideals of socialism and communism.

Despite the contradictions and disagreements, Lenin's legacy and role in creating the first socialist state continue to be the subject of study and debate among historians, political scientists, and philosophers. For many, he remains a symbol of the fight for social justice and radical transformation of society. By contrast, others see in his methods and in the consequences of his policies lessons about the risks of authoritarianism and centralized control.

On a global scale, Leninism inspired many revolutionary movements and regimes in various parts of the world throughout the twentieth century. Countries such as North Korea, China, Cuba, Venezuela, Vietnam, and others relied to varying degrees on Leninist principles to carry out their socialist revolutions and build their government structures.

That included an emphasis on Communist Party leadership, the pursuit of socialism through revolution, and the application of the dictatorship of the proletariat as a way to combat bourgeois elements and hostile external forces.

The global influence of Leninism and its ideas has attracted both admiration and criticism. In some countries, socialist experiments have led to significant social and economic achievements, including improved access to education, health care, and general living standards. However, these experiments were often accompanied by political repression, freedom restrictions, and economic difficulties.

Criticism of Leninism's practical implementation often focuses on centralized leadership, suppression of opposition, democratic principles, and freedom of speech.

Central planning and insufficient market mechanisms led to inefficiency, shortages, and slow economic growth.

In many cases, attempts to build a socialist society were accompanied by massive repression, human rights violations, and the creation of police states.

The legacy of Leninism in the modern world remains complex and contradictory. On the one hand, his ideas continue to inspire left-wing and anti-capitalist movements that genuinely fight for social justice and equality. On the other hand, the twentieth-century experience demonstrates the severe risks and dangers associated with authoritarian socialism, which attempts to radically restructure society without considering democratic norms and human rights.

In many countries of the former Soviet bloc, there has been a rethinking and critical analysis of the Soviet legacy, leading to the abandonment of Leninism as a state ideology and a transition to various forms of democratic governance and market economies. However, in some countries, especially those where socialist and communist parties retain power, the ideas of Lenin and Marxism-Leninism continue to play a significant role in political life and ideology.

In the modern world, Lenin's ideas are being reinterpreted in the context of new social, economic, and political challenges. Some leftist and socialist theorists are exploring how Marxist-Leninist principles can be adapted to globalization, the digital economy, and the environmental crisis, seeking ways to achieve a more just and sustainable social order.

The cultural and ideological legacy of Lenin and Leninism left a deep imprint on the art, literature, cinema, and education of the countries they dominated. Although this legacy is sometimes revised or criticized, its influence on world history and culture remains undeniable.

While leftist and anti-capitalist movements may be inspired by Leninist theory, they often strive for more inclusive, democratic, and diverse forms of social and economic organization. They criticize capitalism and authoritarian tendencies within historical socialist and communist movements, seeking new ways to develop socialism in the twenty-first century.

As the creator of the first state based on Marxist ideology, Lenin left a complex legacy that continues to generate heated debate and varied interpretations. His contributions to the development of Marxist theory and the practice of socialism have profoundly impacted world history, and critical analysis of his ideas and actions provides essential lessons for modern social and political movements.

After coming to power, the Bolsheviks pursued the policy of "military communism," which included the grain requisition from peasants to supply the army and urban population. That caused discontent among the peasants and contributed to the outbreak of peasant uprisings. In 1921, after a large-scale uprising in the Tambov region and a catastrophic famine, the authorities were forced to abandon the policy of war communism and introduce the NEP (New Economic Policy), which restored partial private farming in agriculture.

The October Revolution of 1917 significantly impacted Russia and the world community, leading to many long-term changes in the political, economic, and social structure of many countries.

The revolution led to the overthrow of the Provisional Government and establishment of Soviet power, which marked the end of the monarchy and the beginning of the construction of a socialist state. The Civil War that followed the revolution led to enormous casualties as well as the destruction of the economy and social structure of the country.

New Economic Policy (NEP): In an attempt to restore the economy after the Civil War, the authorities introduced the NEP, partially restoring private property and entrepreneurship in agriculture and some industries. The change in economic policy during industrialization and the collectivization of agriculture led to fundamental changes in the economic and social life of the country.

The revolution and subsequent changes contributed to increased access to education, science, and culture and the development of ideologically charged art and literature.

The October Revolution inspired communist and socialist movements worldwide, especially in Europe and Asia.

The creation of the USSR and the ideological confrontation between the communist bloc and Western democracies became one of the main factors that led to the beginning of the Cold War. The Soviet Union actively supported movements for national liberation in colonial and dependent countries, which contributed to decolonization after World War II. The establishment of Soviet power in Russia and the subsequent formation of the USSR led to a rethinking of international relations and the balance of power in the world. The race to develop new types of weapons in military-industrial complexes significantly influenced scientific and technological progress in the second half of the twentieth century.

Attempts to resolve global conflicts and prevent new wars led to the creation and strengthening of international organizations such as the UN, whose role in the postwar world order became critical. The USSR and post-Soviet Russia played a vital role in the development and implementation of many principles of international law.

The rivalry between the communist and capitalist worlds led to numerous cases of interference in the internal affairs of other countries' support for regimes or opposition groups in "hot spots" of the Cold War. The USSR's policy of economic support and cooperation with developing countries contributed to the formation of new economic ties and development models that differed from Western approaches. That has also contributed to the processes of globalization and changes in the world economic structure.

The Cold War was accompanied by intense cultural exchange and a propaganda war in which both sides sought to demonstrate the superiority of their socioeconomic model and ideology. That competition between ideologies has significantly influenced culture, art, science, and education globally.

Competition in the space race and the development of new military technologies have stimulated research and innovation, which have wide applications in civilian fields, including computer technology, telecommunications, medicine, and transportation.

The October Revolution and subsequent events played a crucial role in shaping twentieth-century world history, defining geopolitical, social, and economic trends that continue to influence international relations and the development of the world community to this day.

The October Revolution dramatically changed Russia's political landscape. It became a beacon for many movements for socioeconomic equality worldwide, leaving behind a legacy that continues to provoke debate and analysis.

After the collapse of the Soviet Union in 1991, many independent states emerged in their former territories. The processes started by the October Revolution largely determined the political and economic foundations of these new countries, their foreign policy orientations, and internal transformations.

The October Revolution inspired the creation and activation of many left-wing movements worldwide, including anti-colonial and civil rights struggles. It also influenced the development of ideologies such as Marxism-Leninism, which became the basis of many national liberation movements.

The revolution led to experimentation with various forms of government management of the economy, including planned economies and collectivization. These ideas influenced economic models in many countries, especially in the search for alternatives to the capitalist system.

Soviet art, literature, cinema, and educational and scientific achievements that emerged after the revolution significantly impacted world culture. The Soviet Union helped spread its cultural and ideological achievements, which led to the formation of a specific idea of socialism in various parts of the world.

The example of the USSR inspired many countries regarding social protection, education, and health care, which led to reforms in these areas. Attempts to create socialist states in various parts of the world were also motivated by a desire for social justice, inspired by key events of the twentieth century that transformed Russia and profoundly impacted global political, economic, and cultural life. The consequences and lessons of the USSR's example continue to be discussed and analyzed in many countries, highlighting the complexity and diversity of its influence on world history.

Contemporary perceptions of the October Revolution vary significantly across countries and cultures, reflecting a wide range of opinions from deep respect and idealization to criticism and condemnation. The legacy of the revolution continues to influence political debate, especially in discussions about socialism, capitalism, and the future of social justice.

The October Revolution contributed to a significant expansion of access to education and science in Russia. This expansion laid the foundation for the scientific achievements demonstrated by the Soviet Union in the twentieth century, which inspired many countries to expand educational programs and scientific research.

The influence of the October Revolution on the formation of the world political landscape of the twentieth century is difficult to overestimate. It led to the formation of many socialist and communist states, a change in the global balance of power, and the development of international relations based on new principles. Even more than a century after the October Revolution, its influence is felt in many aspects of modern life, from political ideologies to social policies and cultural exchanges. This revolution remains a subject of research, debate, and reflection, emphasizing its importance in understanding the past and thinking about the future.

Thus, the October Revolution continues to be an essential element of global historical memory, symbolizing the desire for radical change and embodying hope but also serving as a warning for future generations. Because the October Revolution occupies such an essential place in the history of the twentieth century, its legacy and influence continue to generate keen interest a century later. The event's historical significance explains this interest and how it continues to influence modern political, economic, and social processes in different parts of the world. Modern studies of the October Revolution often acquire a multidisciplinary character, combining historical analysis with political science, sociology, economics, and cultural studies. That allows for a deeper understanding of how the revolution influenced the development of government institutions, economic systems, social structures, and cultural practices.

In the context of globalization, the history of the October Revolution reminds us of the importance of understanding the historical roots of modern international relations and global political processes. By analyzing its implications, researchers can better understand current issues and conflicts related to ideological differences, economic instability, and the desire for social justice.

In an educational context, the study of the October Revolution promotes the development of critical thinking, allowing students to analyze complex historical processes, understand different points of view, and evaluate the consequences of historical events for the present. It also provides an opportunity to discuss significant power, social justice, economic development, and international relations issues.

The cultural legacy of the October Revolution is still visible in literature, art, cinema, and other forms of cultural expression. These works reflect historical events and ideas of the time and continue to inspire contemporary artists and thinkers to create new creative works that address current social and political issues.

Discussions about the legacy of the October Revolution and its significance for the modern world continue in academic circles and public discourse. These discussions often concern questions about the possibility and feasibility of applying the ideas of revolution in modern conditions, as well as what lessons can be drawn from the experience of the Soviet Union to solve current global problems. Particular attention is paid to analyzing the mistakes and achievements of the Soviet model in economics, social policy, management, and international relations.

Political forces of different orientations interpret the legacy of the October Revolution differently, using it to justify their ideological positions and political programs. For some, it remains a symbol of the struggle for social justice and equality; for others, it serves as a cautionary tale about the risks of radical social experiments.

Studying the consequences of the October Revolution on social and economic development allows us to better understand the relationship between political reforms and their long-term socioeconomic consequences. An important aspect is the analysis of how the revolution affected income distribution, access to education and healthcare, and the development of science and technology.

The October Revolution and the subsequent formation of the Soviet Union significantly influenced world history, including decolonization, the formation of Cold War blocs, and the development of international law. Analysis of these aspects helps us understand how 1917 affected international relations and world politics. The legacy of the October Revolution also stimulates ethical and philosophical reflection on the nature of power, the state's role in society, the possibilities and limits of social engineering, and the moral dilemmas associated with revolutionary violence and the pursuit of social justice.

The October Revolution continues to be the subject of active research and debate, providing rich material for analysis in various disciplines. The revolution's legacy has influenced political thought, social movements, culture, and the arts, continuing to generate interest and debate among researchers, policymakers, and the public worldwide.

This extensive legacy and the continuing influence of the October Revolution underscore its significance as a historical moment and a phenomenon that continues to influence modern society and world politics. It remains a living subject of analysis, contributing to a deep understanding of the dynamics of social progress, political power, and the human desire for justice and equality. All of these factors make the study of the October Revolution an integral part of understanding both the past and the present, offering lessons and perspectives for the future development of humanity.

Joseph Stalin
The path to the top of power

Joseph Stalin's path to the pinnacle of power in the Soviet Union was long and complicated, from his early years in the revolutionary movement to his rise to absolute power after the death of Vladimir Lenin in 1924. Stalin's political career was based on specific tactics: cunning, political intrigue, and a ruthless struggle for power, which ultimately allowed him to seize authoritarian control of the USSR and remain in power until he died in 1953.

Born in 1878 in Georgia into a low-income family, Stalin (real name Joseph Dzhugashvili) showed interest in revolutionary activities from an early age. His path to power began with studying at a theological seminary in Tiflis, where he became acquainted with Marxist ideas. He soon left the seminary and devoted himself entirely to revolutionary activities, joining the Russian Social Democratic Labor Party (RSDLP).

During the revolutions of 1905 and 1917, Stalin played an active role, although he was not as prominent as some other revolutionaries. After the October Revolution, he received several important posts in the new Soviet government, including the People's Commissar for Nationalities, which allowed him to gain support from the diverse peoples of the USSR. After Lenin died in 1924, a power struggle began within the party between Stalin and his opponents, including Leon Trotsky, Lev Kamenev, and Grigory Zinoviev. Stalin used his position as the party's general secretary to appoint his supporters to key positions, thus consolidating his power. He skillfully manipulated differences between his rivals, ultimately removing them from power.

By the end of the 1920s, Stalin had effectively established himself as the undisputed leader of the Soviet Union. He initiated a series of political repressions known as the Great Terror, aimed at eliminating any opposition to his rule, including old revolutionaries and party officials, as well as many ordinary citizens. These actions strengthened his power but also led to massive repression and suffering among the population of the USSR.

Stalin's predilection for political intrigue led to ruthless struggle with opponents and the desire for absolute power. His reign profoundly impacted the history of the USSR and world history, leaving behind a controversial legacy that still causes heated debate among historians and political scientists.

Once he established his power, Stalin began implementing ambitious programs for the economic and social development of the Soviet Union, which had far-reaching consequences for both the country and the world.

One of Stalin's key initiatives was the forced collectivization of agriculture, aimed at accelerating the process of industrialization at the expense of agricultural production. This process led to widespread famine, most famously the Ukrainian Holodomor (1932–1933), which led to the deaths of millions. Collectivization also caused widespread discontent among the peasantry and led to a significant decline in agricultural productivity.

In parallel with collectivization, Stalin launched a five-year plan to industrialize the USSR. These plans focused on the development of heavy industry and the defense sector, allowing the Soviet Union to significantly increase its industrial capacity and prepare for the upcoming challenges of World War II.

Stalin's domestic policy was characterized by the continuation and expansion of political repressions in the late 1920s. The Great Terror reached its climax in the late 1930s, when hundreds of thousands of people, including high-ranking military commanders, party leaders, and ordinary citizens, were arrested, tried, and executed. These repressions created an atmosphere of fear and suspicion that permeated all layers of Soviet society.

On the international stage, Stalin sought to secure the Soviet Union from external threats and expand the influence of communism. In 1939, the USSR and Germany signed the Molotov-Ribbentrop Pact, which provided for non-aggression between the two countries and the division of spheres of influence in Eastern Europe. However, in 1941, Germany broke the pact by attacking the Soviet Union, which led to the USSR entering World War II on the Allies' side.

The military successes of the Soviet Union in World War II, including victory in the Battle of Stalingrad and the capture of Berlin, significantly strengthened the international position of the country and Stalin personally as one of the world's foremost leaders. After the war, Stalin played a crucial role in expanding the Soviet Union's sphere of influence in Eastern Europe, laying the foundation for the Cold War between the USSR and the West.

Stalin's legacy remains the subject of intense debate. On the one hand, his reign is associated with industrialization, victory in World War II, and the transformation of the USSR into a superpower. On the other hand, it was marred by mass repressions, famine, political purges, and the creation of a totalitarian regime, the consequences of which are still felt today.

After Stalin died in 1953, the Soviet Union entered a new era marked by attempts to preserve his legacy while introducing reforms and distancing itself from his widespread and profound influence.

After Stalin, Nikita Khrushchev came to power and initiated the process of de-Stalinization, which reached its apogee in his "secret speech" at the 20th Congress of the CPSU in 1956. In this speech, Khrushchev criticized Stalin's cult of personality and the ongoing repressions, which became a signal for the weakening of the repressive apparatus and the rehabilitation of many victims of Stalin's purges. This period in the history of the USSR is often called the "Thaw" due to the relative weakening of political control and censorship and increased cultural and scientific exchange with the West.

Internationally, Stalin's death led to changes in the Cold War between the Soviet Union and the West. Although tensions and competition remained, periods of dialogue and détente began as both sides sought to reduce the risk of nuclear conflict. Stalin's foreign policy, expanding and supporting communist movements worldwide, was revised in favor of a more moderate and strategic approach to expanding the influence of the Soviet Union.

After Stalin's death, attempts at reform began in the USSR economy. Steps were taken to soften some of the harsher aspects of Stalin's economic policies, including partially allowing private initiative in agriculture and reducing the emphasis on heavy industry in favor of consumer goods and services. However, despite these reforms, many of the structural problems of the Soviet economy that had been laid down during Stalin's time remained unresolved. Continued centralization, inefficiency, and lack of incentives to innovate ultimately led to the stagnation that characterized the subsequent decades of Soviet history.

Stalin's legacy continues to be deeply controversial in modern Russia. For some, it remains a symbol of the greatness of the country, victory in the Great Patriotic War, and industrialization. By contrast, for others, it is associated with repression, terror, and mass casualties. Questions of assessment and interpretation of the Stalinist period remain the subject of political and historical discussions, reflecting the complexity and contradictions of this figure in the history of Russia and the world.

From the CHEKA to the FSB

State security agencies played a crucial role in the history of Soviet Russia and the Russian Federation, providing support to the existing regime through intelligence, counterintelligence, internal security, and political repression. These bodies underwent several renamings and reorganizations during the 20th and early 21st centuries, reflecting changes in the political structure and priorities of the state. Below is a brief overview of the role and evolution of these structures.

VChK - All-Russian Extraordinary Commission

Created in December 1917, immediately after the October Revolution, the Cheka, under the leadership of Felix Dzerzhinsky, became the first Soviet state security agency. The Cheka fought counter-revolution, sabotage, and profiteering, often resorting to brutal methods, including mass arrests, executions, and the creation of a system of concentration camps.

GPU - State Political Administration

In 1922, the Cheka was transformed into the GPU (State Political Administration) under the NKVD (People's Commissariat for Internal Affairs) of the RSFSR. The NKVD continued the functions of the Cheka but with broader powers and structure.

OGPU - United States Political Administration

In 1923, the GPU was transformed into the OGPU, which in 1934 became part of the NKVD of the USSR. The OGPU was responsible for internal and external security, which was vital in organizing mass political repressions.

NKVD – People's Commissariat of Internal Affairs.

In 1934, the OGPU was included in the structure of the NKVD, which became one of the most influential bodies in the USSR, responsible for state security, internal affairs, and the management of the GULAG camps. Under the leadership of Nikolai Yezhov and Lavrentiy Beria, the NKVD carried out massive political repressions known as the Yezhovshchina.

After the death of Stalin and the reorganization of state structures, the NKVD was divided. In 1946, the MGB (Ministry of State Security) was created, which dealt with issues of state security, and other functions of the NKVD were transferred to new ministries.

In 1954, the MGB was transformed into the KGB (Committee of State Security), one of the world's most famous and influential intelligence and counterintelligence services. The KGB was involved in various tasks, from combating domestic political dissent to espionage and influence operations abroad. After the collapse of the Soviet Union in 1991, the KGB was divided into several separate departments. In 1995, the FSB (Federal Security Service) was created as the primary agency responsible for Russia's internal security, counterintelligence, and the fight against terrorism. The FSB is the successor to the KGB and plays a crucial role in ensuring the national security of modern Russia.

All of these organizations contributed to the establishment and maintenance of the Soviet regime, using a variety of methods to combat natural and perceived threats to internal and external security. Their activities significantly impacted the history of the Soviet Union and modern Russia, causing controversy and debate regarding their role in public life and politics.

The influence of state security agencies on society and politics in the Soviet Union and post-Soviet Russia can be divided into several key aspects, reflecting their role in maintaining power, shaping foreign policy, and influencing public opinion.

State security agencies were a tool in the hands of the Soviet government to maintain political and social control across the USSR. They carried out political repression against real and imaginary opponents of the regime, including political dissidents, "enemies of the people," religious figures, and national minorities. These actions included arrests, interrogations, torture, deportations, and executions. The GULAG system became one of the most sinister symbols of a repressive apparatus in which millions of people were held in labor camps and subjected to ruthless working and living conditions.

Internationally, the KGB and its predecessors conducted active intelligence activities to gather intelligence, conduct influence operations, and support pro-communist movements and regimes worldwide. During the Cold War, KGB agents battled Western intelligence agencies in complex espionage and counterintelligence operations. These actions significantly influenced Soviet foreign policy and global dominance strategy.

Influence on public opinion and culture: State security agencies also actively monitored media outlets, literature, art, and science to prevent the spread of "ideologically harmful" views and ideas. Through censorship, propaganda, and public opinion monitoring, they influenced the formation of loyalty to the Soviet regime and communist ideology. This influence extended to all aspects of cultural life, from cinema and theater to literature and education.

After the collapse of the Soviet Union, the FSB became the key state security agency in the Russian Federation, inheriting many of the functions and methods of the KGB. The FSB plays a central role in ensuring internal security, combating terrorism and extremism, and conducting counterintelligence operations. At the same time, it is also involved in protecting state secrets cybersecurity and monitoring compliance with information technology and communications legislation. The FSB is actively shaping Russia's foreign policy strategy through intelligence activities and support of Russian interests abroad.

One of the priority areas of activity of the FSB in the post-Soviet period was the fight against terrorism, especially after a series of terrorist attacks in Russia in the late 1990s and early 2000s. The FSB carries out operations to prevent terrorist acts, eliminate terrorist groups and networks, and investigate terrorist crimes.

In the era of globalization and the development of digital technologies, the FSB pays special attention to information security issues, including the protection of state information resources, the fight against cybercrime, and control over the dissemination of information on the internet that may threaten national security.

The FSB also plays a significant role in Russian domestic politics, providing stability and support to the current government. That includes measures to prevent and suppress political extremism, monitor the activities of opposition groups and organizations, and participate in anti-corruption activities.

In the international arena, the FSB continues the traditions of Soviet foreign intelligence, collecting information important for Russia's national security and interacting with foreign partners on issues of combating international terrorism, drug trafficking, and other transnational threats.

The activities of the FSB, like those of its predecessors, cause ambiguous reactions both within the country and at the international level. Human rights organizations and international observers have expressed concern about allegations of human rights violations, abuse of power, and the use of the FSB for political repression against opposition and government critics.

The state security bodies of the Soviet Union and the Russian Federation have played and continue to play a crucial role in maintaining the state system and ensuring the external and internal security of the country. However, their activities are often accompanied by controversy and criticism from the public and the international community over their practices, including accusations of human rights violations, abuse of power, and politically motivated repression.

The FSB and its predecessors' influence on Russian society is profound and multifaceted. On the one hand, these structures help ensure the safety of citizens and protection from terrorist threats and cyberattacks. On the other hand, their actions raise concerns about restricting civil liberties and rights, increasing government control over personal life, and curbing political activity.

At the political level, the FSB and its predecessors significantly influence Russia's domestic and foreign policy. They form national security strategies in domestic politics, fight extremism and radicalism, and conduct anti-corruption campaigns. In international politics, the FSB's activities aim to protect Russia's state interests, cooperate with foreign intelligence services in the fight against global threats, and provide intelligence support for Russian foreign policy.

At the international level, the activities of the FSB and its predecessors are viewed through the prism of global security and cooperation in the fight against international terrorism. At the same time, foreign governments and international organizations closely monitor the FSB's actions to ensure human rights and compliance with international standards.

The role of the FSB and its predecessors in the history of Soviet Russia and the post-Soviet Russian Federation is the subject of lively debate and research. These security agencies have remained and continue to be among the most potent instruments of government management and control, contributing to the country's stability and security and raising questions about the balance between security and freedom, power, and responsibility to society.

Nikita Khrushchev

After Stalin's death, Nikita Khrushchev came to power and initiated the process of de-Stalinization, which culminated in his "secret report" at the 20th Congress of the CPSU in 1956.

General Secretary of the CPSU Central Committee Nikita Khrushchev, for the first time openly (for the delegates of the congress), cited the horrifying facts of the genocide of the Soviet people and the role of Stalin in that matter. In concentration camps subordinated to the KGB, people who disagreed with the authorities were exterminated. At times, unfounded accusations, torture, and execution of millions of prisoners were used. The KGB was used as a brutal instrument of power to keep the population at bay. At the 20th Congress of the CPSU in February 1956, Nikita Khrushchev delivered a historic speech officially entitled "On the Cult of Personality and Its Consequences." In this report, Khrushchev criticized the cult of personality of

Joseph Stalin and revealed a number of his crimes against the Soviet people and the party. This speech was an essential moment in the history of the Soviet Union since it was the first time that the repressions carried out under Stalin were condemned at such a high level.

Khrushchev blamed Stalin for the massive repressions that led to the arrest, torture, execution, and exile of millions of people, many of whom were innocent. He mentioned unfounded accusations, fabricated trials, and the culture of fear and suspicion that Stalin created within the country and the Communist Party.

The KGB (Committee for State Security), the successor to the NKVD and other repressive bodies, was indeed used as a tool to suppress political dissent and control the population during and after Stalin's time. The repressions affected broad sections of the population, from high-ranking party functionaries to ordinary citizens.

Khrushchev's report shocked the congress delegates and had long-lasting consequences at home and abroad. It marked the beginning of a process of de-Stalinization aimed at condemning Stalin's crimes and removing some of his management methods. However, a complete break with repressive practices did not occur immediately, and many aspects of the Soviet political system remained unchanged.

That period in the USSR's history has still caused much controversy and discussion among historians, politicians, and the public, emphasizing the difficulty of assessing historical figures and events.

Khrushchev's report at the 20th Congress of the CPSU catalyzed many changes in the Soviet Union and foreign policy.

Also, it influenced the perception of the USSR in the world. Reaction to the report was mixed and had a wide range of consequences:

The process of de-Stalinization included debunking Stalin's personality cult, renaming cities and places associated with his name, and playing down his role in the history of the USSR. Many victims of Stalin's repressions began to be rehabilitated. Thousands of political prisoners were released from camps, and many had their names posthumously restored. Khrushchev tried to reform the governance of the country and the Communist Party, pushing for more excellent collective leadership and a reduction in bureaucracy.

The report deepened divisions between the Soviet Union and China, led to a split in the global communist movement, and played a significant role in the Cold War. The revelation of Stalin's crimes helped some Western countries enter into dialogue with the USSR, which led to a temporary easing of tensions during the Cold War.

In Soviet society, the report sparked widespread debate and rethinking of Soviet history, although these discussions were often held behind closed doors due to restrictions on freedom of speech. The revelation of Stalin's repression also inspired the dissident movement in the USSR, which demanded deeper reforms and freedoms.

Although Khrushchev's report was critical in recognizing and condemning Stalin's crimes, many critics note that it did not go far enough in democratizing the country and reforming the political system. Moreover, after Khrushchev's resignation in 1964, many of his initiatives were canceled or slowed down by his successors, which shows the complexity and contradictions of the de-Stalinization process.

The process initiated by Khrushchev's report to the 20th Congress of the CPSU profoundly impacted subsequent generations in the Soviet Union and beyond, influencing the political landscape, cultural perception, and historical scholarship. Although Khrushchev's reforms were controversial and inconsistent, they laid the foundation for a more open discussion of political and social problems in the USSR. That included limited criticism of the internal party bureaucracy and attempts to reform economic policy.

The report contributed to the "thaw" in Soviet culture, which allowed more significant discussion of historical and social issues and the emergence of works previously banned by censorship. This time became a renaissance for many art, culture, and literature areas.

Despite temporarily easing tensions between the USSR and the West, the split between the Soviet Union and China intensified the ideological confrontation within the communist bloc, which had long-term consequences for world politics. The report changed the world's perception of socialism and communism, sparking debate about the nature and development of socialist states and the moral and ethical implications of using power for social engineering.

Khrushchev's report and subsequent archival discoveries stimulated new research into the period of Stalin's rule, including analysis of the causes and consequences of mass repression. The introduction of new facts and interpretations contributed to the emergence of revisionist movements in historical scholarship, sparking debate about the Stalinist regime's causes, nature, and consequences.

Khrushchev's secret report at the 20th Congress of the CPSU remains one of the most significant moments in the history of the 20th century, embodying the attempt of the Soviet leadership to rethink the history of the country and its future. Its consequences are still felt today in Russia and abroad, emphasizing the complexity of historical reflection and reassessment of the past. The report influenced political reforms and cultural life in the USSR. It contributed to changes in the foreign policy situation, especially in relations between East and West during the Cold War.

The discovery of facts about Stalin's repressions and subsequent research also led to changes in education and historical science approaches in Russia and other countries. The curriculum introduced new information about the Stalinist period, allowing generations of students to better understand their country's history. Discussions about the Stalinist regime and its legacy, as well as assessments of the actions of Nikita Khrushchev, continue to play an essential role in modern public and political discourse in Russia and beyond. These debates reflect different points of view on the history of the Soviet Union and its place in world history, as well as disagreements about the path of modern Russia and its identity. The process of reinterpretation of the Stalinist period and de-Stalinization shows the difficulties that society faces when trying to reconstruct historical memory, especially when it concerns tragic and controversial aspects of the past. The importance of open access to archival materials and freedom of research in this context cannot be overstated.

The legacy of the 20th Congress of the CPSU and Khrushchev's report remain the subject of active research and discussion. The memory of Stalin's repressions and efforts to comprehend them and rehabilitate the victims continue to influence the processes of formation of identity and political culture in post-Soviet states. Thus, Nikita Khrushchev's secret report became an essential milestone in the history of not only the Soviet Union but also the entire world, having a profound impact on many aspects of international politics, social thought, and culture. It continues to generate interest and serve as a subject for reflection on the importance of historical truth, methods of governing society, and the consequences of political decisions.

A discussion of the implications of the Khrushchev Report and its impact on modern society cannot be complete without considering the ongoing efforts to research and understand the Soviet period of history. These efforts have several key aspects:

In the post-Soviet era, interest in a detailed study of the Stalinist regime increased, leading to the publication of many research works based on previously inaccessible archival materials.

The Khrushchev Report and the de-Stalinization events that followed became an essential part of the post-Soviet rethinking of history, which continues to this day. That process involves academic research, education, public debate, memorialization, and political debate. It reflects the complexity of the interaction between historical memory, identity, and politics, emphasizing the need for continued dialogue about the past to understand the present and build the future.

Dialogue between countries with experience in overcoming complicated historical legacies can contribute to developing effective strategies for social reconciliation and recovery after tragedies.

Continuing dialogue about the past, especially about such complex and painful aspects as Stalin's repressions, requires the joint efforts of society, the state, historians, and educational institutions. That contributes to a deeper understanding of history and plays an essential role in shaping public values based on respect for human rights and democratic principles.

Continuing dialogue about the past requires openness, a willingness to have difficult conversations, and acknowledging painful aspects of history. Only by working together can we achieve a deep understanding of the past, ensure justice for victims, and lay the foundation for a bright future in which the lessons of history serve as a warning against repeating mistakes and as a basis for building a society based on respect, tolerance, and protection of human rights.

Khrushchev condemned the use of terror, which became a political tool of the Stalinist regime, and pointed out the destructive consequences of Stalin's personality cult for Soviet society and government. These actions were presented as a betrayal of the ideas of socialism and the October Revolution.

Khrushchev's report was not made public then and was distributed mainly behind closed doors among the party elite, although its contents soon became known and received wide international publicity. This speech strengthened a critical view of the Stalinist era in the USSR and the international community.

* * *

The collapse of the USSR in 1991 became a crucial event in world history at the end of the 20th century. That was the process of collapse of the Union of Soviet Socialist Republics (USSR); as a result, the state, which occupied a sixth of the landmass and included fifteen union republics, ceased to exist.

The USSR's collapse began in the 1980s against serious economic problems, political stagnation, and the strengthening of national movements within the country. The following factors played an essential role in this process:

Reforms launched in the mid-1980s by CPSU General Secretary Mikhail Gorbachev aimed to modernize the Soviet economy and political system. However, they also increased criticism of the authorities, public consciousness growth, and the activation of national movements.

The late 1980s and early 1990s were marked by the growth of nationalist sentiments in several union republics. That led to mass protests demanding greater autonomy or complete independence from Moscow.

The USSR faced a deep economic crisis, manifested in commodity shortages, stagnation of production, and growing external debt.

The internal political struggle between supporters of preserving the USSR and those who advocated its reform or its collapse weakened the central government and destabilized the situation.

The unsuccessful attempt of conservative elements in power to preserve the USSR with the same powers of centralized power only accelerated the process of disintegration.

On December 8, 1991, the leaders of Russia, Ukraine, and Belarus signed an agreement that began the process of the collapse of the USSR and the creation of the Commonwealth of Independent States (CIS).

On December 25, 1991, Mikhail Gorbachev announced his resignation as President of the USSR. On the same day, the Soviet flag was lowered over the Kremlin, symbolizing the end of the Soviet Union.

The collapse of the USSR had far-reaching consequences not only for the former Soviet republics but also for the entire world. These consequences are also felt in the modern geopolitical environment, economics, culture, and international relations.

All fifteen republics that were part of the USSR declared their independence and became sovereign states. That required them to form their state institutions, economic systems, and foreign policy directions.

The transition to a market economy proved difficult for most newly independent states. Privatization, inflation, unemployment, falling living standards, and economic recession became a reality in the 1990s.

In some regions, such as Chechnya in Russia, Nagorno-Karabakh in Armenia and Azerbaijan, and Transnistria in Moldova, armed conflicts have broken out over national self-determination and territorial disputes.

The collapse of the USSR eliminated the main threat of nuclear war and led to the end of the Cold War between East and West. That opened the way to new international relations and cooperation.

Without the Soviet Union as a counterweight, many Eastern European countries and former Soviet republics sought to join

NATO and the European Union, significantly changing the political map of Europe.

The collapse of the USSR and the transition to market economies in the former Soviet republics accelerated globalization, making the world economy more interconnected.

The collapse of the USSR led to questions of control over nuclear weapons, which ended up on the territory of several newly independent states. Signing treaties on non-proliferation and reducing nuclear arsenals was an important step. Independence gave impetus to the development of national cultures.

The collapse of the USSR had many significant consequences, both for the former Soviet republics and the world.

After the collapse of the USSR, fifteen new independent states appeared on the world's political map, each beginning its development path with its own political and economic system.

Many new countries faced severe economic problems, including inflation, unemployment, and falling living standards. Transitioning from a planned economy to a market economy was painful and lengthy.

The collapse of the USSR also led to the emergence and aggravation of numerous interethnic and territorial conflicts, some of which still continue.

The end of the Cold War and the collapse of the Soviet Union led to dramatic changes in the system of international relations. The United States remained the only superpower that influenced political and economic dynamics worldwide.

Former Soviet republics and Eastern European countries sought integration into Western political and economic structures, leading to the eastward expansion of NATO and the European Union.

Many countries that emerged from the ruins of the USSR began the democratization process, although the success of these reforms was uneven. Some countries have established authoritarian regimes, while others have made significant progress toward democracy.

In many new states, reviving national languages, cultures, and traditions subject to assimilation or restrictions during the Soviet period began. Thus, the consequences of the collapse of the USSR turned out to be multifaceted and continue to influence world politics, economics, and culture.

Putin

Path to Power

Vladimir Putin's path to power in the Russian Federation is one of the most significant political phenomena in recent history. His career spans the transition period after the collapse of the Soviet Union when Russia was searching for its new identity on the world stage and its path of internal development. This is a brief overview of the critical stages of Putin's career and his rise to power.

Vladimir Putin was born on October 7, 1952, in Leningrad (now St. Petersburg). After graduating, he entered the Leningrad State University Faculty of Law, from which he graduated in 1975. After university, Putin joined the KGB, serving in various countries, including the German Democratic Republic in the 1980s.

In the early 1990s, returning to Leningrad, Putin went to work in the city administration, where he quickly rose through the ranks under the leadership of Mayor Anatoly Sobchak. There is little doubt that the KGB service blessed this transition to the Leningrad city administration. Putin was involved in foreign relations and investment issues, allowing him to establish many contacts domestically and abroad.

In the mid-1990s, Putin was invited to Moscow, where he began working in the administration of President Boris Yeltsin. His career in the federal government began as Deputy Director for Presidential Affairs. He then moved to more senior positions, including leadership of the Federal Security Service (FSB) and the Security Council of the Russian Federation—a brilliant career for an ordinary FSB officer.

In August 1999, Putin was appointed prime minister of Russia, and already in December of the same year, after the resignation of Boris Yeltsin, he served as interim president of Russia. In March 2000, he was elected president, beginning his first four-year presidential term.

After two presidential terms (2000-2008), under the Constitution of the Russian Federation, Putin could not run for a third term in a row and became prime minister, transferring presidential powers to Dmitry Medvedev. In 2012, there was a reshuffle, as chess players say, and Putin was again elected president, followed by several more terms, the last of which began in 2018. Since 2024, Putin has been president of Russia for more than twenty years.

Throughout his rule, Putin has focused on strengthening state sovereignty, rebuilding the economy after the crisis of the 1990s, raising living standards, and returning Russia to Great Power status on the international stage. His rule was met with criticism for tightening domestic policies, restricting the press and political freedoms, and for Russia's actions on the international stage, including the conflict in Ukraine.

Putin's rise to power and his long tenure in top government positions reflect complex dynamics in Russian politics and society, and his personality and actions continue to resonate widely at home and abroad.

In March 2024, Vladimir Putin was once again re-elected President of the Russian Federation, and his activities continue to influence the political situation both within the country and in the international arena. The question of his future largely depends on internal and external political factors and the major decisions of Putin himself.

Over time, various scenarios may occur. For example, if the constitutional order changes, Putin may decide to step down as president at the end of his term. Possible other options include moving to other government or public leadership positions.

At the same time, the political system in Russia continues to be influenced by various factors, including the level of support among the population, the actions of the opposition, foreign policy pressure, and other factors. Therefore, the future of the political situation in Russia remains the subject of widespread debate and forecasts.

The attack on Ukraine in the context of modern events can be explained by several key events over the past few decades.

One of the most significant events was the annexation of Crimea by Russia in 2014. After major protests in Ukraine led to the overthrow of pro-Russian President Viktor Yanukovych, the Russian military seized Crimea, held a referendum on annexing the peninsula to Russia, and then annexed it. Many countries around the world condemned this act, considering it a violation of international law, and Ukraine continues to insist on its sovereignty over Crimea. Another significant development is the armed conflict in eastern Ukraine, which began in 2014. Pro-Russian separatists, with Russian support, took control of large territories in the Donetsk and Lugansk regions. This conflict has resulted in thousands of deaths and injuries, as well as severe geopolitical and humanitarian consequences.

Many countries and international organizations have condemned Russia's actions in Ukraine and have taken many measures, including imposing sanctions against Russian officials and companies. The West provided support to the Ukrainian army and economic assistance to Ukraine. However, the conflict remains relevant, and efforts to resolve it continue.

The attack on Ukraine had a significant impact on international relations and the geopolitical situation. That led to deteriorating relations between Russia and the West, increased American and European support for Ukraine, and changes in many countries' defense and foreign policies.

In general, the attack on Ukraine and subsequent events left a deep mark on the history of modern Europe and world politics, and these events continue to remain one of the main problems and challenges for the international community. Following the attack on Ukraine and subsequent events, the conflict in eastern Ukraine has continued for several years, causing suffering to the local population and increasing tensions in the region. Important political events took place in Ukraine, including presidential and parliamentary elections. In 2019, Vladimir Zelensky was elected president of Ukraine, promising to fight corruption and solve the conflict in the east. This period was also marked by increased attention to reforming the country, promoting economic development, and strengthening ties with the West.

The international community continued to actively support Ukraine and mediate in resolving the conflict. However, the issue of regaining control over the territories lost by Ukraine and restoring the country's territorial integrity remains one of the main challenges for the Ukrainian government and the international community.

Events in Ukraine also had far-reaching consequences for regional international relations and security. The conflict has heightened tensions between Russia and the West, brought attention to security and stability issues in Eastern Europe, and become the focus of debate and diplomatic efforts to address global issues.

In general, the situation in Ukraine continues to be complex and dynamic, and conflict resolution remains one of the international community's priorities in ensuring peace and stability in the region.

The attack on Ukraine and the armed conflict in the east of the country have created a tense situation. On the line of contact between the Ukrainian Armed Forces and the separatists, armed clashes periodically resumed, which led to casualties and destruction in the conflict zone.

Ukraine continued to strive for integration with the European Union and NATO, signing agreements on cooperation and interaction. That caused some concern in Russia, which feared a loss of influence in its "near abroad." The international community continued to discuss sanctions against Russia in connection with its actions in Ukraine. Sanctions remained one of the tools that Western countries used to put pressure on Russia and support Ukraine.

Ukraine also faced internal problems, including corruption, economic difficulties, and political instability. The Ukrainian government has taken steps to combat these problems, but a solution still seems like a distant prospect.

On February 24, 2022, Russia attacked Ukraine. A full-scale military invasion began on three fronts: from the Russian Federation, Belarus, and the annexed Crimea. This war, which has claimed thousands of lives and led to millions of refugees, has been going on for more than two years. The conflict between Ukraine and Russia remains one of the leading international crises of our time, attracting the close attention of the world community. This year, the situation at the front continues to be tense, with active hostilities and humanitarian problems.

At least 23,600 civilians have been killed or wounded since the conflict began, according to the UN. The humanitarian situation remains critical, with significant damage to civilian infrastructure, including homes, schools, and health facilities.

The year 2023 was characterized by military successes for Ukraine, including attacks on airfields in Russia and Crimea, but these actions did not lead to significant changes at the front. At the same time, internal disagreements within the Ukrainian leadership and doubts about the continued support of the West raised additional concerns.

The international community continues to provide humanitarian assistance to the affected population and support Ukraine's quest for peace and sovereignty. An essential part of the effort was the Black Sea Grain Initiative, which ensures the export of Ukrainian grain to maintain global food security. The situation in Ukraine remains complex and dynamic, requiring careful monitoring and an adequate international response to find ways to resolve the conflict and minimize its consequences for the civilian population.

The war in Ukraine has been raging for two years. If Russia wins, the Western world needs to prepare. The predator will never have enough. He fears and hates everyone. Instinct pushes him to attack first. His only chance of survival is to dominate everyone. His fevered imagination paints pictures of enemies thirsting for his blood. It is not necessarily this mad beast that is scary. The worst thing is that Western politicians believe the beast can be tamed. The West must unite and destroy this rabid and sick animal. No reason, agreement, contract, or promise will work. The obsessed Fuhrer Hitler is still alive in the memory of generations. He ridiculed the naivety of his opponent, who was ready to accept any agreement. Fear of the threat of war will lead to war. Today's Russia is far superior to Hitler both in military power and in its readiness to unleash a universal conflagration.

Europe is thinking about a peace treaty between Russia and Ukraine. No one wants a new world war in the center of Europe. The latter has its problems with new immigrants from Asia and Africa. Other cultures and religions are destabilizing the situation in the once well-fed, calm life of the "Old World." There is understandable fear for their children's future in this new reality, a dead end that will be difficult to work around. The lack of peace and stability makes every European want peace at any price. Today, Ukraine is a bargaining chip, a price that a predator demands. It has always been so. It will be so in the future.

Iran

After the overthrow of the Shah, significant changes took place in Iran, profoundly impacting the country's political, social, and economic life. The overthrow of Shah Mohammad Reza Pahlavi occurred during the Islamic Revolution of 1979, which led to the creation of the Islamic Republic under the leadership of Ayatollah Ruhollah Khomeini.

After the overthrow of the Shah, a theocratic state was created in Iran: the country went from a monarchy to an Islamic republic with a unique form of government, where the final word in many matters remains with the highest religious authority (currently the Supreme Leader), which is final in most aspects of the state and social structure.

In 1979, a new constitution enshrined Islamic governance principles and the legal system and introduced the Supreme Leader position.

The religious influence of Islam grew and began to play a central role in public life, influencing education, legislation, and everyday aspects of citizens' lives.

Women's rights were limited, although they actively participated in the revolution. However, a strict dress code was imposed on them after its success, and many rights and freedoms were curtailed.

The government took control of the oil industry, which had previously been in the hands of foreign companies. Iran has faced international sanctions, especially from the United States, which have impacted the country's economy.

Relations between Iran and the West, especially the United States, deteriorated after the seizure of the American embassy in Tehran in 1979, leading to a protracted crisis.

Iran has become an active participant in regional conflicts, supporting allies in Syria, Lebanon, Iraq, Yemen, and other countries. These changes have created significant challenges for Iran and provided the country with opportunities to strengthen its sovereignty and regional influence.

After an initial change following the 1979 Islamic Revolution, Iran experienced periods of liberalization and reform under presidents such as Mohammad Khatami and Hassan Rouhani, who sought to improve relations with the West and liberalize domestic policies. However, these periods often alternated with moments of tightening control by conservative forces within the country.

Despite the restrictions, Iran has a vibrant civil society that periodically demonstrates its dissatisfaction with government policies, economic conditions, and social restrictions through mass protests.

Besides the oil industry, Iran is trying to develop other economic sectors, such as agriculture, technology, and tourism, to reduce its dependence on oil revenues. Iran's economy continues to suffer from international sanctions restricting its trade and investment. Temporary sanctions relief under the 2015 nuclear deal (Joint Comprehensive Plan of Action) was rescinded again following the US withdrawal from the deal in 2018.

Iran's nuclear program remains a subject of international concern and negotiations. Iran maintains its nuclear program is for peaceful purposes only, while other countries have expressed concerns about the possibility of Iran developing nuclear weapons.

Iran is actively involved in regional politics in the Middle East, supporting allies in Syria, Iraq, Yemen, and Lebanon. This involvement is causing tension among several regional countries, including Saudi Arabia, Israel, and the United States.

Iran faces serious environmental problems, including water scarcity, desertification, and air pollution, especially in large cities such as Tehran. These challenges require an integrated approach to managing resources and developing sustainable solutions to support the country's environmental well-being and public health.

Iran has demonstrated significant progress in science and technology despite international sanctions, especially in medicine, nanotechnology, and space. The country strives to develop domestic technological potential and reduce dependence on foreign technologies.

Developing a digital economy is also a priority for Iran, focusing on developing startups and the IT sector, contributing to job creation and innovation in various fields.

Iran's cultural life, including literature, cinema, music, and the visual arts, remains rich and varied. Iranian films regularly receive international awards, indicating the country's highly sophisticated cinematic art.

Censorship and restrictions on freedom of speech remain serious problems, and restrictions on the press and the internet have drawn criticism from international human rights organizations.

Iran places great importance on education, having one of the highest adult literacy rates in the region. Higher education and scientific research are also reasonably high, thanks to numerous universities and research institutes.

The country faces challenges due to the migration of educated professionals abroad searching for better opportunities, known as "brain drain."

Iran has an extensive healthcare system providing a significant level of medical services. The country has significantly improved public health and reduced child mortality in recent decades.

Iran has undergone profound changes since the overthrow of the Shah and continues to adapt to new challenges and opportunities. The country remains a complex international player that has influence in regional affairs in the Middle East. It continues to develop its domestic political, economic, and cultural life despite internal and external problems.

Relations between Iran, its proxies, and international allies—the Houthis in Yemen, Hezbollah in Lebanon, Hamas in Gaza, Iraq, Syria, Russia, and North Korea—are vital aspects of its foreign policy and regional influence. These ties allow Iran to strengthen its position in the region and beyond despite international sanctions and diplomatic isolation. Here is an overview of the main areas of Iran's engagement with these groups and countries:

Proxy Groups: Iran supports the Houthis (officially called Ansar Allah) by providing them with military assistance, including weapons and training. The support is part of a broader regional standoff with Saudi Arabia, which is waging a military campaign against the Houthis in Yemen.

Hezbollah is considered one of Iran's closest allies in the region. Iran provides financial, military, and political support to Hezbollah, which plays a significant role in Lebanese politics and armed conflicts in the Middle East.

Relations between Iran and Hamas have had their ups and downs, especially since the Syrian civil war. Iran continues to support Hamas, providing financial assistance and weapons to fight against Israel.

Iran exerts significant influence in Iraq through its support of Shiite militias and political parties. These groups play a crucial role in Iraqi politics and security, allowing Iran to increase its influence.

Iran is a crucial ally of Bashar al-Assad's Syrian government, providing military support, including ground troops, advisers, and militias. This support helped Assad maintain power during the civil war.

Cooperation with Russia and North Korea allows Iran to strengthen its defense capabilities and circumvent international sanctions. In the case of Russia, this cooperation also has a regional dimension, especially in Syria, where both countries support the Assad regime. Cooperation between Iran and North Korea is also characterized by cooperation, especially in the military and nuclear fields. Both countries face international sanctions and isolation, working together to circumvent these restrictions. North Korea has reportedly provided Iran with technology to develop ballistic missiles and may have assisted in its nuclear program.

Iran's relationships with its proxies and international allies reflect a complex network of interactions that plays a crucial role in its regional and global influence strategy. These relationships strengthen Iran's position in the Middle East and cause tension and conflict with other states seeking to control its influence. Engagement with Russia and North Korea underscores Iran's desire to work with other isolated countries to resist Western pressure and bolster its defense and technological capabilities.

All these interactions and relationships significantly impact regional and global stability. Iran's support for proxy groups increases its influence in the region but also leads to tensions and conflicts with other countries, especially Saudi Arabia, Israel, and the United States, which view Iran's actions as a threat to their interests.

The current confrontation between Iran and Israel is one of the most significant and long-lasting regional conflicts in the Middle East. This confrontation has many dimensions, including political, strategic, ideological, and religious.

Ideological and religious differences:
Since the Islamic Revolution of 1979, Iran has declared its strong support for the Palestinians and has repeatedly called for the destruction of the State of Israel. That is in sharp

contrast to Israel's policy of maintaining its sovereignty and security, as well as its position on the Palestinian issue.

Military and strategic rivalry:
Iran and Israel are involved in indirect military rivalry, which manifests itself through the support of proxy groups and military operations. Israel accuses Iran of trying to develop nuclear weapons and of supporting terrorist groups such as Hezbollah in Lebanon and Hamas in the Gaza Strip, which pose a threat to Israel's security. In response, Israel conducted military operations against Iranian targets in the region, especially in Syria, where Iran supports the Assad government.

Regional alliances and influence:
Iran is seeking to expand its influence in the Middle East by supporting allied groups and governments in countries such as Syria, Iraq, Lebanon, and Yemen. Israel, in turn, seeks to balance this influence by strengthening its relations with other Arab states, as evidenced by recent normalization agreements with some of them (for example, the Abraham Accords).

Iran's Nuclear Program

Iran's nuclear program remains a central element of tension between the two countries. Israel, which has its nuclear arsenal (although it does not officially recognize it), views Iran's possible acquisition of nuclear weapons as a threat to stability and peace in the Middle East. That has led to ongoing Israeli calls for the international community to tighten sanctions against Iran and even threats of military intervention to stop Iran from developing nuclear weapons.

In the international arena, Iran and Israel are actively seeking to gain support for their positions from other countries and international organizations. This confrontation is manifested in the exchange of accusations and attempts to influence international opinion on issues important to both countries.

Overall, the confrontation between Iran and Israel is deep-rooted and multifaceted, covering a wide range of political, strategic, and ideological differences. This confrontation has a significant impact on regional stability in the Middle East and requires careful balancing of foreign policy by many international players.

Iran plays a crucial role in supporting proxy forces in the fight against Israel, using the groups Hezbollah and the Houthis Ansar Allah in Yemen. Iran prefers to operate behind the scenes and through these armed groups, viewing them as part of a "sacred axis of resistance" to American and Israeli authorities. These groups act under Iranian foreign policy and strategic goals; for example, the Houthis in Yemen attack commercial and military ships in the Red Sea, which is in line with Iranian interests. Hezbollah, a Lebanese Shiite group, is one of Iran's key allies in the region. Before the Syrian civil war, Hezbollah positioned itself as a force fighting Israel. Syria served as a transit point for supplies of military equipment from Iran to Hezbollah. After the outbreak of the civil war in Syria, Hezbollah actively supported the Assad regime, which caused a change in the perception of the group among Sunnis. Hezbollah has also expressed solidarity with Hamas and exchanged blows with Israel, raising the possibility of broader conflict if Israeli troops enter the Gaza Strip.

The Islamic Revolutionary Guard Corps (IRGC) considers Lebanon the front line in the fight against Israel, using the country's territory for possible rocket attacks on Israel, even against the will of official Beirut. That demonstrates how Iran uses proxy groups and allied territories to project its influence and achieve strategic goals in the region despite risks to local populations and regional stability.

Hezbollah leader Hassan Nasrallah did not rule out the possibility of a full-scale war between Israel and Lebanon, emphasizing that such a scenario is entirely accurate, and warned the Israeli army against actions on the Lebanese front. Nasrallah stressed that Israel must recognize the reality of the threat of a full-scale conflict and that a preemptive strike on Lebanon would be the "stupidest mistake" in Israeli history. In response, Israeli Prime Minister Benjamin Netanyahu said Hezbollah's decision to enter the war would be "the mistake of its life," promising strikes of "unimaginable force."

Analysts warn that a potential war between Israel and Hezbollah could be significantly more dangerous and bloodier than the current conflict with Hamas, pointing to severe consequences for the entire region. This situation highlights the complexity and instability of the situation in the Middle East, where tensions between Israel and its neighbors continue to rise, creating risks of broader conflict.

Biden's America

2020-2024

From 2020 to 2024, Joe Biden served as the 46th President of the United States of America, succeeding Donald Trump. Biden, a longtime member of the Democratic Party and former vice president under Barack Obama (2009–2017), focused his campaign on critical issues, including combating the COVID-19 pandemic, economic recovery, climate change, social equality, and rebuilding US alliances internationally.

On climate issues, Biden announced the US return to the Paris Climate Agreement. One of Biden's first decisions after taking office was to revoke the permit for the Keystone XL pipeline, which would have transported oil from Canadian sandstones to Texas. The decision comes as part of his pledge to combat climate change and shift to cleaner energy sources.

The Biden administration passed the $1.9 trillion American Rescue Plan to support American citizens and small businesses due to the economic damage caused by the COVID-19 pandemic. The plan included direct payments to citizens, increased unemployment benefits, and financial support for small businesses.

In April 2023, Joe Biden announced his intention to run for a second term as President of the United States in the 2024 elections. However, the outcome of these elections and the final decision on whether he will seek a second term will depend on the vote results.

An assessment of Biden's presidency, as for any president, depends mainly on political views, individual beliefs, and interpretation of his administration's achievements and failures. US public and political discourse offers a wide range of opinions regarding his leadership of the country.

Biden's critics point to various aspects of his policies and governance that they believe have harmed the country. That includes his approaches to economic policy, border management, COVID-19 response, and foreign policy. They may argue their case by pointing to high inflation, immigration issues, or energy decisions that they believe undermine national security and economic stability.

Joe Biden, who served as Barack Obama's vice president from 2009 to 2017, is often associated with the policies and achievements of the Obama administration. Since being elected president in 2020, Biden has primarily positioned himself as a continuator of some aspects of Obama's policies, particularly in health care, climate change, and foreign policy. Here are some critical areas Biden is following or expanding on Obama administration policies.

Biden advocated for strengthening and expanding the Affordable Care Act (ACA), which was passed during the Obama administration.

Like Obama, Biden is focused on combating climate change. He announced the US return to the Paris Agreement immediately after taking office and proposed an ambitious program to achieve carbon neutrality by 2050.

Biden seeks to rebuild alliances and partnerships that he believes have been undermined in previous years. He emphasized the importance of international cooperation and multilateral approaches to solving global problems, which was reminiscent of Obama's approach.

The Biden administration is pushing for more humane immigration policies that also reflect the aspirations of the Obama administration, albeit with some changes and clarifications.

Biden is focused on economic recovery from the COVID-19 pandemic, including significant investments in infrastructure and technology, which also reflects the Obama administration's interests in economic development and innovation.

However, there are also differences in both administrations' approaches due to changes in the global political, economic, and social environment, as well as the unique challenges faced by the Biden administration, including the COVID-19 pandemic and its aftermath. Biden has also proposed and implemented several initiatives that reflect his priorities and views on governing the country.

During the two terms of the Obama administration, Barack Obama and Joe Biden maintained a close working and personal relationship when Biden served as vice president. This experience undoubtedly influenced Biden as a politician and his approach to governing as president. However, the extent to which Obama directly influenced Biden's decisions during his presidency may be less obvious and direct.

Biden's experience in the Obama administration gave him a unique perspective and understanding of federal governance that could be used in his presidential decisions. Biden may also have sought advice from Obama on critical issues, given their long-term partnership and Obama's experience as president. Given their similar political views and values, it can be assumed that Obama's ideological influence and approach to governing remain relevant to Biden. That could include a general focus on health care, climate change, economics, and foreign policy.

Despite the influence and experience gained while working with Obama, Biden has demonstrated a willingness to advance his priorities and initiatives that may differ from or complement the Obama administration's approaches. Examples include his approach to the COVID-19 pandemic, economic recovery, and infrastructure investment.

Biden faced unique challenges, such as the COVID-19 pandemic and its social and economic impacts, that required specific solutions different from those faced by the Obama administration. Ultimately, Obama's experience and approach certainly influenced Biden.

The year 2024 is a US presidential election year and will determine who is president for the next four years. Biden announced his election participation, hoping to receive a majority of votes and be elected to a second term. His opponent, like four years ago, is Donald Trump. The fight will be uncompromising.

It is of course impossible to accurately predict the winner of the 2024 US presidential election. The main political opponents—the Democratic and Republican parties—are actively preparing for the elections, nominating various candidates and formulating their strategies. Various internal factions within both parties, including more radical groups, make the race particularly unpredictable.

The 2024 election will be the first after the Electoral College votes were redistributed based on the 2020 US Census results. This redistribution of electoral votes will affect the outcome of the election, and the current political map of the United States shows that some states, such as the Rust Belt and Sun Belt states, are vital battlegrounds, making them essential to candidates' strategies.

Determining each party's candidates includes primaries and caucuses in different states, where voters decide who will represent their party in national elections. It is important to note that the winner of primaries and caucuses receives the support of a certain number of delegates, which is only a promise of support at the national level.

Given these aspects, the election outcome will largely depend on the current political environment, including intra-party competition, national and international issues, and how candidates can mobilize voters in key states.

Shimon Garber

Afterword

In the current climate of geopolitical tensions, technological advances, and environmental challenges, the future of our world appears to be heading toward a period marked by significant transformation. Experts from various think tanks and institutions have expressed their views on what could shape the international system soon.

One of the main themes is the changing nature of global trade and inequality, the impact of cyberspace and new technologies, and the critical importance of addressing climate change and the transition to sustainable energy sources. These factors are expected to redefine competition and conflict, challenging the traditional role of nation-states in the international system. The decline of multilateralism, exacerbated by the US-China rivalry, underscores the need for a new approach to global governance that can effectively address transnational challenges.

The rivalry between the US and China, especially in the economic sphere and their influence in the Indo-Pacific region, is becoming a defining feature of global geopolitics. While maintaining its military and cultural influence, the United States is believed to lag behind China regarding economic relations within the region. These dynamics are critical because they could shape the geopolitical landscape for decades. The gap in economic diplomacy, highlighted by the US absence from major trade agreements such as RCEP and CPTPP compared to China's active participation, suggests a shift in the balance of power.

Let's look ahead to 2025-2030. The four scenarios assume varying degrees of US and Chinese influence, the resilience or weakening of both countries in the wake of COVID-19, and their bilateral interactions. Neither of these scenarios assumes full cooperation between the US and China; however, they highlight opportunities for selective cooperation on global issues where interests coincide. The future geopolitical order is expected to be characterized by weak multipolarity, with the influence of other major powers such as India, Japan, and European countries becoming more significant. This emerging landscape suggests that no single nation will dominate, leading to a more fragmented world order in which regional powers will play a key role.

In summary, the world is at a crossroads, facing complex economic, technological, and environmental challenges that require a radical rethink of international governance and cooperation. The future will likely be marked by messy multilateralism, the dynamics of competition between major powers, and the need for innovative approaches to global governance that can navigate the intricacies of the 21st century. The path forward will require flexibility, collaboration, and a commitment to addressing fundamental issues that transcend national borders.

The events in mid-April 2024 decisively changed the course of world events, and the world community, lulled by seeming local conflicts, suddenly woke up from the dormant lethargy of an established peaceful confrontation. Russia, with a consistency worthy of better use, is destroying the infrastructure and population of Ukraine. The European Union and the United States are helping the Ukrainians to weaken Russia any way they can and still remain on the sidelines—for fear of being drawn into a military confrontation. The rest of the world condemns aggression, and the remaining observers are ready to support the winner.

Iran, having decided that the time has come to show who solves problems in Asia and the world, has moved from passively supporting its proxies—XAMAS in the Gaza Strip, Hezbollah in Lebanon, the Houthis in Yemen, and the obedient leaders of Syria— announced its decision to punish the state of Israel, which has long and publicly warned the world community about the danger from Iran, which is preparing to create atomic weapons. On the night of April 13–14, 2024, Iran directly attacked Israel. The armada of unprecedented simultaneous power consisted of advanced combat vehicles, including 170 drones, 30 cruise missiles, and more than 120 ballistic missiles. Tehran called it self-defense and a reaction to the Israeli air force strike on the Iranian consulate in the Syrian capital in April 2024.

Iran: "We attacked the Zionist regime following Article 51 of the UN Charter (attack in self-defense) after the attack on Damascus. We warn Israel against any military action. We will legally respond to aggression against our interests and territorial integrity."...

Permanent Representative of the Islamic Republic to the UN Amir Said Iravani.

The Israel Defense Forces reported intercepting 99 percent of Iranian missiles and drones. Several Iranian missiles hit Navatim Air Base in the Negev Desert without causing any damage.

The armed forces of the United States, United Kingdom, France, and Jordan took part in the defense of Israel. The White House strongly condemned Iran's actions, announcing consultations with G7 allies to develop a diplomatic response to Iran's attack on Israel.

Israel called on the international community to impose sanctions against Iran in response to the missile strike. Israel also intends to respond to Iran's strike, considering various options for retaliation. The international community fears a regional war in the Middle East that could escalate into a major war, threatening to turn the Arab world into a battlefield between Israel and Iran. The leading countries of our world may be drawn into this confrontation. The specter of World War III is already frighteningly close.

Over the five to six thousand years of world civilization, humanity has experienced many wars, from predatory to religious ones, from colonial to ideological ones, from liberation to socialist ones, the First World War 1914–1918 and Second World War 1939–1945. Humanity is inventing more advanced weapons to destroy each other. The pinnacle of human genius was the invention of the atomic bomb. This terrifying weapon of destruction of its species, Homo sapiens, will sooner or later fall into the hands of religious or ideological fanatics who hate those who do not share their views. Humanity has already entered the threshold of mutual destruction and self-destruction. On the night of April 13, 2024, ultra-religious Iran sent an armada of unprecedented power to destroy the state of Israel. The attack was repulsed with the help of Israel's allies. It is inconceivable to think of what could have happened if an Iranian missile had hit an Israeli nuclear reactor. Is it the beginning of the end or just the end of a stupid kind of ape-man?

The civilization of the species Homo sapiens began with the construction of houses of worship (ziggurats), and today's descendants of those who believe in higher powers seek to destroy all living things, hoping to survive with the help of these significantly higher powers. Ideologies are the same religions, but the concept is built on a different principle. The ideologists of Marxism-Leninism, Stalinism, Maoism, and other isms strive for world domination and the destruction of all dissenters. Many of these countries already have atomic weapons and will not hesitate to use them.

There is nothing worse than religious and ideological fanatics who are ready for self-destruction in the name of their faith or ideals.

Does this mean that humanity is doomed? Only time will tell. We can only hope that we do not live to see this more than regrettable moment.